Trevor and Duncan Smith are father and son respectively, and this is their second co-written work. Their first was the highly successful *South and West Yorkshire Curiosities*, published by the Dovecote Press in 1992.

Trevor Smith, of Scottish extraction, was born in Sheffield in 1921. He has had a varied career, including some eight years of teaching and many more in public and University libraries. He has a lifelong interest in freelance writing and photography and for some considerable time has been compiling a list of curiosities of the British Isles.

Duncan Smith, now 32, was born and raised in Sheffield. From the age of ten he has been an avid collector of all things historical, going on to read ancient history and archaeology at Birmingham University. A keen traveller, gardener and book collector, he currently works in the publishing industry.

Frontispiece
*Yorkshire's oldest Lighthouse on the headland
at Flamborough (see no 17).*

North and East Yorkshire Curiosities

Duncan and Trevor Smith

THE DOVECOTE PRESS

For Mary, Catherine, Adrian and Eva

Also available by the same authors:
South and West Yorkshire Curiosities

'If you have ever wondered about an unusual building or folly, or like exploring man's eccentricities, this book is a must.'
Dore to Door

'. . . an entertaining look at 82 of the county's odder corners.'
The Sheffield Star

First published in 1993 by the Dovecote Press Ltd
Stanbridge, Wimborne, Dorset BH21 4JD

ISBN 1 874336 09 1

© Duncan and Trevor Smith 1993
Phototypeset in Times by The Typesetting Bureau
6 Church St, Wimborne, Dorset
Printed and bound in Singapore

Contents

Acknowledgements

Many people have helped us in the compilation of this book and we would like to express our thanks to the following. First and foremost David Burnett of The Dovecote Press for his enthusiasm and for giving us the chance to publish our work. Also Simon Laffoley for his companionship on many journeys into the field and his invaluable help with map-reading, and to Alex Hart and Pauline Hollow for typing the manuscript.

For permission to take photographs we thank: William Harrison of The Whitby Literary and Philosophical Society (Whitby Museum), The National Trust (Monks Chapel at Fountains Abbey), English Heritage (Byland Abbey, Mount Grace Priory, Richmond Castle, Rievaulx Abbey, Wharram Percy and Whitby Abbey), Rebecca Morgan of The Landmark Trust (Beamsley, Cawood, Fylingthorpe and Richmond), Stephen Halstead (Arnford), Mrs C Wilkinson (Masham) and Mr A Lambert (Aysgarth). Also Celia King for her sketch of Skipton Castle.

We all owe a debt of gratitude to The Landmark Trust who have made it their job to lovingly restore many of the country's unusual buildings, which may now be rented as self-catering accommodation with a difference. For their Handbook please contact The Landmark Trust, Shottesbrooke, Maidenhead, Berks. Tel. 0628 825925.

Finally, thanks to the following who were more than happy to spare a few minutes talking about this book: Bridget Yelland of Alne, Helen Walasek of Whitby Museum, Doug Morton of Beck Hole, Victor Povid, Eva Holland and Lawrence Bowkett.

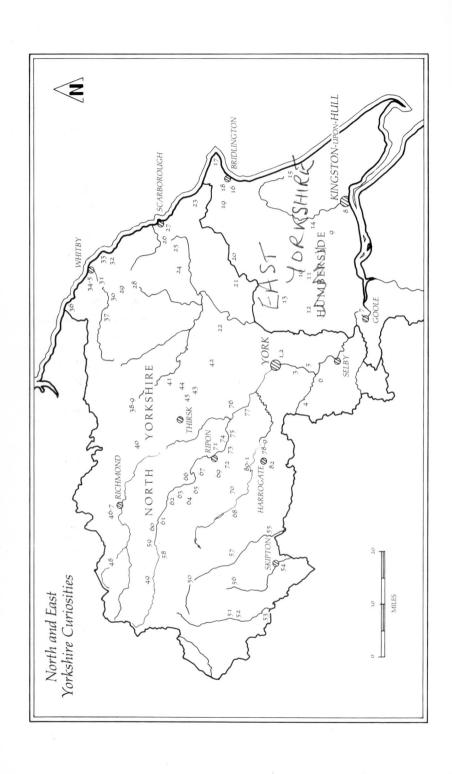

North and East
Yorkshire Curiosities

Introduction

The term "curiosity" is of necessity a subjective one. The criteria adopted here is that it need not be necessarily unique but ought to be rare, as well as historically or architecturally unusual. It can be important or trivial, famous or little known, but must have an interesting story which evokes bygone days in Yorkshire.

Our journey will take us through the varied landscapes of North Yorkshire and North Humberside, starting off in the Plain of York and crossing into the gently rolling Wolds and flat country of Humberside to the south-east. Then we travel up the wild Yorkshire coast and across the bleak, heather-clad North Yorkshire moors, and finally across the rural Dales and into Pennine country.

This present volume forms a sequel to our *South and West Yorkshire Curiosities* and thus completes our coverage of the entire county. In dividing our entries for the present volume we have distinguished between North Yorkshire and North Humberside, reflecting today's modern boundaries. However, our reference to "East Yorkshire" on the cover demonstrates the strong desire to return to the old Ridings of Yorkshire whereby North Humberside would revert to East Yorkshire – time will tell!

Many of the sites described can be seen easily all year round. Others, however, are stately homes and museums with opening hours and admission prices. The odd one is even on private land in which case permission must always be sought. In the case of churches, it is best to visit on Sunday as many are now sadly locked during the week.

Directions have been kept brief and all map references refer to the Ordnance Survey 1:50,000 Landranger Series. A glance at our map will show that the sites are numbered in a broadly anti-clockwise direction beginning in York. At the end of each entry is a selection of other sites described in the book which lie within a ten mile radius. Occasionally, as is the case with curious graves, a number of examples are brought together from all around the area, forming a thematic journey in itself.

Duncan and Trevor Smith
Sheffield, 1993.

1 A Window as Big as a Tennis Court

Position: York (N Yorks)
O.S. Map: York & surrounding area: Sheet No. 105
Map Ref: SE 604/524
Access: The Minster dominates the city centre skyline and lies at the end of Stonegate.

York Minster is the largest Gothic church in England, indeed in Europe. Completed in 1480, it is the fifth edifice to have been built on the site, standing as it does on the Roman military headquarters. There is no trace of the Saxon Minster of King Edwin, destroyed in 1069, but

The Great East Window of York Minster.

there are Roman remains in the Undercroft Museum below the Minster. Here can been seen a Roman tile with a dog's pawprint on it, whilst outside the porch is a reconstructed 22 feet tall Roman column.

The Minster is thought to contain as much as half an acre of glass in its windows. This includes the famed East Window (1408), which, at 78 by 36 feet, is as big as a tennis court and one of the biggest in the world. Another, the so-called 'Five Sisters Window', or the 'Jewish Window', was probably financed by the Jews of the city, although their generosity did not prevent a later outbreak of anti-Semitism.

Other curiosities include the choir screen with its carvings of the Kings of England, Archbishop Thomas's tomb with its effigy of his dog Scamp and a medieval Latin inscription which sums up the Minster's appeal – 'the building of buildings, just as the rose is the flower of flowers!'

A more recent rarity is the Astronomical clock, a unique War Memorial to Yorkshire's many fallen airmen of World War II. The astral and zodiacal dials have relevance to local flight navigation and the small left-hand dials convert hours to degrees as used by navigators. A Book of Honour lists their names together with illustrations of their aircraft.

Places of Interest in the Neighbourhood
2. York's Street Curiosities
3. The Canal Owner's Banqueting House
5. The Viking Boat on a Church Door
76. Maiden's Garlands

2 York's Street Curiosities

Position: York (N Yorks)
O.S. Map: York & surrounding area: Sheet No. 105
Map Ref: SE 60/52

One of York's curious legacies are the numerous sculptures, signs and other items of 'street furniture' which can still be spotted by the observant visitor today. These include the following: 1. Stonegate: outside No.33 is a little, red chained devil, a reminder that the shop was once a printer's, 'printer's devils' being the small boys used to fetch and carry type. 2. Stonegate: outside the Starre Inn is a 'gallows sign', a signboard running from one side of the street to the other. 3. Lendal: outside a tobacconist's is a life-size figure of Napoleon. Carved in 1880 it is a rare effigy trade sign, once offering a pinch of snuff to passers-by. 4. Low Petergate: on the corner is a carved Indian boy used as a trade sign to identify the building as a tobacconist's to the illiterate. 5. High Petergate: on a wall can be seen an old 'fire mark', with a cross-

The 'Printer's Devil' outside a shop in York's Stonegate.

The Red Indian outside a shop in York's Low Petergate.

keys design, designating that this building was guaranteed a fire service should it catch fire. 6. Coney Street: two carved cats are attached to the upper storey of a shop frontage and are said to have frightened away rats from the nearby riverside. They were put up in the 1920's by Sir Stephen Aitcheson, owner of a chain of grocery stores. 7. Coney Street: outside the ruined St Martin-le-Grand church is a huge clock topped by the figure of an admiral taking sights with his sextant. 8. St Leonards Place: on the right-hand side of the door knocker of the Red House is a rare 'link extinguisher'. This is a metal cone used in the days before street lighting to extinguish torches (or 'links'). 9. Bishopthorpe Road: an original red-and-white striped barber's pole advertising the fact that barbers originally doubled as doctors if necessary. 10. Lendal Bridge: an unusual Victorian civic fountain dated 1880 at which not only passers-by but also their pet dogs could drink!

Places of Interest in the Neighbourhood
1. A Window as Big as a Tennis Court
3. The Canal Owner's Banqueting House
5. The Viking Boat on a Church Door
76. Maiden's Garlands

3 The Canal Owner's Banqueting House

Position: Naburn (N Yorks)
O.S. Map: York & Surrounding area: Sheet No. 105
Map Ref: SE 594/445
Access: Naburn is 4 miles south of York on the B1222 and the Banqueting House is beyond the village to the south next to the weir and caravan park.

Historically the city of York was a major port for sea-going vessels and in 1462 a charter under Edward IV placed the River Ouse and its tributaries under the control of York Corporation. However, during the eighteenth-century, a series of navigation acts began to undermine this monopoly as the rivers Aire, Calder and Derwent were made navigable

The Ouse Navigation trustees Banqueting House at Naburn Lock.

to the coast. In response, considerable effort was spent on deepening the water level at York which was often too shallow at low tide. Similarly an act in 1727 permitted jetties to be built towards the deeper parts of the river, and in 1757 a weir and lock were built at Naburn. The latter increased the draught in York by some 1 ½ metres. Despite the fact that York's navigational prosperity continued to decline the Corporation saw fit to indulge themselves in what, for the time, was a piece of true architectural folly.

In 1823, adjacent to the lock, they squandered no less than £2,742 on a 60 feet long Banqueting House where the Ouse Navigation Trustees could meet. Such was the outcry that 10 years later when the Municipal Corporation Act was being set up, the building was put forward as an example of the old Corporation's financial mismanagement. The building with its huge doorway leading to the dining-room on the right and the caretakers' room on the left continues something of its original usage today as it is now a restaurant!

Alongside the Ouse in York itself can be found numerous interesting canalside buildings, such as the Bonding Warehouse built in 1875 beside Skeldergate Bridge (SE 603/513); it too now used as a restaurant.

Places of Interest in the Neighbourhood
1. A Window as Big as a Tennis Court
2. York's Street Curiosities
4. The Virgin Viaduct
5. The Viking Boat on a Church Door
6. Where Humpty Dumpty Fell

4 The Virgin Viaduct

Position: Tadcaster (N Yorks)
O.S. Map: York & surrounding area: Sheet No. 105
Map Ref: SE 485/438
Access: Tadcaster is 9 miles south-west of York on the A64 and the viaduct crosses the River Wharfe just north of the town, adjacent to the road bridge.

'The Virgin Viaduct' at Tadcaster is so-called because the York-Leeds railway for which it was built never actually arrived. This was due to the collapse of the York and North Midland Railway Company in 1849. However, the viaduct did see some usage in supplying coal to the steam-powered corn mill (1883) built on the site of an old watermill adjacent to the viaduct. The mock-Romanesque mill, with its castellated tower, was then converted to a coal-fired power station in 1903 by John Smith, the famous local brewery. This provided power to the brewery and the town until its closure in the 1950's, since when it has been a warehouse.

Places of Interest in the Neighbourhood
1. A Window as Big as a Tennis Court
2. York's Street Curiosities
3. The Canal Owner's Banqueting House
5. The Viking Boat on a Church Door
6. Where Humpty Dumpty Fell

The so-called 'Virgin Viaduct' over the Wharfe at Tadcaster.

5 The Viking Boat on a Church Door

Position: Stillingfleet (N Yorks)
O.S. Map: York & the surrounding area: Sheet No. 105
Map Ref: SE 593/410
Access: Stillingfleet is 6 miles south of York on the B1222 and St Helens church is in the centre of the village.

Most of St Helens church dates from the thirteenth to fifteenth centuries but the core of the buildings is Norman, the north and south doorways being twelfth century. The carving on the latter is particularly fine and the door itself (now inside the church) retains its original wrought iron strapwork. The finest example of such still 'in situ', it may be Saxon in date. It is thought to be the work of a blacksmith versed in the Norse tradition because it depicts a Viking-style long ship complete

Ironwork on the old church door at Stillingfleet.

with 'steer-board' and dragons head prow. The door hinges are also terminated with characteristic dragons heads and there are two figures, perhaps representing Adam and Eve.

In the graveyard is a memorial to eleven choristers drowned when their boat capsized after a carol service in 1833.

Places of Interest in the Neighbourhood
1. A Window as Big as a Tennis Court
2. York's Street Curiosities
3. The Canal Owner's Banqueting House
4. The Virgin Viaduct
6. Where Humpty Dumpty Fell

The gatehouse of the Archbishop's Palace at Cawood.

6 Where Humpty Dumpty Fell

Position: Cawood (N Yorks)
O.S. Map: York & surrounding area: Sheet No. 105
Map Ref: SE 575/375
Access: Cawood is 5 ¼ miles north-west of Selby on the B1223.

The quaint, red-tiled village of Cawood once boasted its own castle overlooking the river, and was an inland port for the distribution of building stone. Kings and Queens were entertained here and it later became the palace of the Archbishops of York. The latter were like a local royal family whose opulence drew the cream of English nobility. A banquet staged by Archbishop George Neville reputedly led to the consumption of 1,000 sheep, 4,000 pigeons and 3,000 cold custards, to name but part of the menu.

Today only the tall Gatehouse from the time of Archbishop Kempe (1426-51) remains, with its oriel windows amd wide archway built from the local creamy limestone. The rest is gone and one can only imagine the scene when in 1530 the Earl of Northumberland demanded the palace keys and arrested Thomas Wolsey, once Henry VIII's most powerful favourite, for high treason. Wolsey, hoping to become Archbishop of York, had become something of a favourite in the town and his abrupt departure caused considerable sadness. Lest we forget him, Wolsey's humiliation has filtered down through history into a well-loved nursery rhyme. It is he who is the Humpty Dumpty who had a great fall and could not be put back together again by the King's men! The castle now belongs to the Landmark Trust who have renovated it as one of their unusual properties to rent.

Places of Interest in the Neighbourhood
1. A Window as Big as a Tennis Court
2. York's Street Curiosities
3. The Canal Owner's Banqueting House
4. The Virgin Viaduct
5. The Viking Boat on a Church Door.

7 A Unique Way to Export Coal

Position: Goole (N Humberside)
O.S. Map: Market Weighton & surrounding area: Sheet No. 106
Map Ref: SE 745/233
Access: Goole is situated at the entrance to the Humber estuary and the docks lie just south of the town centre.

Although Goole lies in South Humberside, and is therefore strictly out of the geographical scope of this book, we have chosen to include it here because it played a vital part in Yorkshire's recent history.

The docks at Goole owe their existence to the construction of the Aire and Calder Navigation (canal) which gave Leeds vital access to the sea. In the 1820's the canal company built a new stretch of canal from the River Aire at Knottingley to the then hamlet of Goole beside the River Ouse. A new port was thus created allowing coal to be brought to the sea from the coal fields of South Yorkshire. The coal arrived in small barges called 'Tom Puddings' – iron tubs carrying 35 tons of coal each. These were linked together in a chain and hauled by tug to Goole docks. There they were raised on a special hydraulic hoist, turned upside down and emptied directly into the holds of waiting ships, like puddings being turned out onto a plate. The coal could then be exported. This unique transportation system was instigated in the 1860's having been pioneered by W. H. Bartholomew, the canal company's engineer.

Despite opposition from the nearby docks at Hull, Goole flourished and in 1848 became the eastern port for the Lancashire and Yorkshire railway, helping it prosper throughout the nineteenth-century.

Places of Interest in the Neighbourhood
No other sites lie within a 10 mile radius of Goole.

✓8 Monument to the Slave Emancipator

Position: Kingston upon Hull (N Humberside)
O.S. Map: Kingston upon Hull & surrounding area: Sheet No. 107
Map Ref: TA 098/288
Access: Kingston upon Hull lies at the end of the M62 and A63 on the
north bank of the Humber estuary. The Wilberforce Monument is in
Queens Gardens and the Town Docks Museum is in Queen Victoria
Square nearby. Wilberforce House is at 25 High Street and is open all
year round except Saturday.

Hull, or more correctly Kingston upon Hull, was the birth place of
William Wilberforce (1759-1833) whose campaigns led to the abolition
of the slave trade. He is celebrated here by a 90 feet high Doric column
erected in 1834 by public subscription, the year after his death.

The Wilberforce Memorial Monument in Kingston upon Hull.

Wilberforce House was where William was born. It is the oldest surviving example of the prosperous, brick-built merchants' houses which lined the old High Street and is unique in having a front garden. It and the adjoining houses are now a museum commemorating Wilberforce and contain items connected with his life and work. These include his books, diaries and his favourite Chippendale chair. Some of the rooms are furnished with period style furniture, silver and costumes.

Of great interest also is the Town Docks Museum housed in the former Hull Dock Company offices. This domed building, constructed in 1871, was once the hub of Hull's dockland and is typically Victorian in its solid and elegant construction. It contains displays on all aspects of Hull's sea-going trade from prehistoric times to the present day, including the development of trawling and whaling. In the seventeenth and eighteenth century fishermen sailed from here to the waters around Greenland and Spitsbergen in search of whales, a valuable source of lamp oil and lubricants.

Places of Interest in the Neighbourhood
9. Yorkshire's Last Complete Windmill
14. England's Largest Parish Church

Yorkshire's last working windmill at Skidby.

9 Yorkshire's Last Complete Windmill

Position: Skidby (N Humberside)
O.S. Map: Kingston upon Hull & surrounding area: Sheet No. 107
Map Ref: TA 021/334
Access: Skidby Mill is on a minor road to the east of the village off the A164, 5½ miles north-west of Kingston upon Hull.

The earliest windmills were called 'Post Mills', comprising a small wooden hut pivoted atop a sturdy vertical post. This allowed the entire structure to be turned to face the wind. By the seventeenth century brick towers were used and only the roof cap was turned. Finally in the eighteenth century a smaller set of sails ('fantail') was added behind the main sails (or 'sweeps') which automatically turned the sails into the wind. The slender form of Skidby Mill is of this latter type, set on a low hill in the rolling East Yorkshire Wolds.

Built in 1821 it is the only fully working survivor of the many windmills that once operated here in the nineteenth century. It is seven storeys high and coated in protective blacktar which contrasts with its white-painted windows. The lowest point reached by its four huge sails deliberately passes in front of a projecting balcony. From here the miller would adjust the shutters of each sail according to the strength of the wind.

Skidby Mill continued in commercial use until 1954 after which it was renovated by Beverley Rural Council and opened as a tourist attraction, where stone-ground wholemeal flour is still produced.

Places of Interest in the Neighbourhood
8. Monument to the Slave Emancipator
14. England's Largest Parish Church

10 Fonts of Curious Wisdom

Position: Goodmanham (N Humberside)
O.S. Map: Market Weighton & surrounding area: Sheet No. 106
Map Ref: SE 889/432
Access: The Village of Goodmanham lies 1 ½ miles north-east of
Market Weighton.

The Old East Riding of Yorkshire is home to a series of richly carved
fonts, and All Saints Church at Goodmanham lays claim to the most
ornate of all. Thought to have been made on the eve of the Reformation
it is inscribed 'Without Baptysm no soull ma be saved'!

Equally curious are four crudely yet boldly carved fonts which seem to
form a group. In St Nicholas at North Grimston (100: SE 842(678) 5
miles south-east of Malton is a font depicting Christ and his Apostles
eating the Last Supper, complete with rolls, fish and goblets of wine.
The font in St Mary's at Cowlam (101: SE 966/655) 2 miles east of
Sledmere shows two grappling wrestlers whilst at St Peter's in Langtoft
(101: TA 008/670) 5 miles north of Driffield can be seen St Lawrence
being tortured on a gridiron. This font was removed from a deserted
village at Cottam, one of many such sites in the area. Finally at St
Mary's in Kirkburn (106: SE 980/551) 3 miles south-west of Driffield
there are depictions of the Baptism of Christ and St Peter being given
the keys of Heaven.

This group of primitive sculpture dates to the eleventh-century and
shows the tenacity of Anglo-Saxon traditions in this rural area.

Places of Interest in the Neighbourhood
11. Memorials to Yorkshire Giants
12. The Sundial Cottage
13. Grave Concerns!

11 Memorials to Yorkshire Giants

Position: Market Weighton (N Humberside)
O.S. Map: Market Weighton & surrounding area: Sheet No. 106
Map Ref: SE 877/418
Access: Market Weighton is 9½ miles west of Beverley on the A1079

In the churchyard of All Saints lies buried William Bradley. Born in 1787 he was the thirteenth child of a local butcher. His siblings were all of normal size but he is said to have weighed a stone at birth and to have added almost a stone each year until his death aged 33. By this time he weighed in at 27 stone. He was 7 feet 9 inches tall and had legs nearly four feet long! One authority at the time spoke of him as being the tallest man ever to have been born in Britain. There is a plaque on the wall of the local cycle shop giving his vital statistics. One of his boots is in a Hull Museum and his special chair can been seen in the Londesbrough Arms public house.

Swainby (93: NZ 478/022) 9 miles north-east of Northallerton is a fourteenth-century village which became a mining community in the nineteenth-century. Close by is the tiny hamlet of Heathwaite which produced a woman called Elizabeth Harland who died in 1812 aged 105, and Henry Cooper who was the world's tallest man in 1890. He was 8 feet 6 inches high and worked in a circus, but died young at 32.

Places of Interest in the Neighbourhood
10. Fonts of Curious Wisdom
12. The Sundial Cottage
13. Grave Concerns!
14. England's Largest Parish Church

The plaque to the Market Weighton giant.

12 The Sundial Cottage

Position: Seaton Ross (N Humberside)
O.S. Map: Market Weighton & surrounding area: Sheet No. 106
Map Ref: SE 778/416
Access: Seaton Ross is 6 miles west of Market Weighton and the Sundial Cottage is on the main street.

Sundials are certainly curious bygones in the sense of their having being replaced by other methods of timekeeping, and our region is fortunate in its number and variety of survivors.

The biggest and most spectacular is the one on a cottage wall at Seaton Ross – in fact with a diameter of 12 feet it is the largest in Britain. It was constructed by William Watson (1784-1857), farmer and sundial enthusiast. His keenness is celebrated on a memorial in St Edmunds churchyard which is inscribed: 'At this church I so often with pleasure did call, that I made a sundial upon the church wall.'

Places of Interest in the Neighbourhood
7. A Unique Way to Export Coal
10. Fonts of Curious Wisdom
11. Memorials to Yorkshire Giants

The famous Sundial Cottage at Seaton Ross.

13 Grave Concerns!

Position: Pocklington (N Humberside)
O.S. Map: Market Weighton & surrounding area: Sheet No. 106
Map Ref: SE 803/490
Access: Pocklington is 13 miles east of York on the A1079 and B1246

North Yorkshire and North Humberside have more than their fair share of curious graves of which a selection is given here.

Of those people who came to an early and tragic end: at Pocklington church there is a plaque outside the east wall of the chancel to the 'Flying Man' who lost his life in 1733 when he slid down a rope from the top of the church to an inn opposite as a stunt; Rudston (101: TA 098/678) churchyard contains the touching life-size statue of a young boy in school uniform who died in 1955; Kirkby Malham (98: SD 894/610) has an epitaph to a knight and his lady who 'died from overwork' after reaping an entire corn field in one day; at Chapel-le-Dale (98: SD 738/772) a plaque in St Leonards church records those who perished during the construction of the famous Settle – Carlisle railway, completed in 1876; and at Towton (105: SE 485/394) there is a cross marking the Battle of Towton which took place on Palm Sunday 1461 and became England's bloodiest battle.

Those graves commemorating unusual achievements include: at Spofforth (105: SE 365/511) in All Saints Church north of the chancel is the grave of 'Blind Jack Metcalfe of Knaresborough' (1717-1810) the great road and bridge builder; in All Saints at Cawood (105: SE 578/379) is a monument to George Mountain who rose from poverty to become Archbishop of York in 1628, dying a few hours later; in St Peter and St Paul's at Pickering (100: SE 799/840) is a plaque to a father and son who helped plan the American city of Washington; and in All Saints at Thornton-le-Dale (100: SE 838/832) is the grave of Matthew Grimes, who guarded Napoleon at St Helena and was a bearer at his funeral.

Some graves reflect people's interests during their life: at Kildwick (104: SE 012/459) is the organ-shaped grave of John Laycock, the first man to build this instrument; a headstone in York cemetery is in the shape of a car complete with number plate; and in St John's churchyard at Sharow (99: SE 328/722) is the pyramidal grave of Charles Piazzi Smyth, famous for exploring the Great Pyramid at Giza in Egypt.

The greatest age on a grave is at Bolton-on-Swale (99: SE 252/992) where Henry Jenkins was buried in 1670 aged 169! He was said to have been swimming in the River Swale at 100 and a fisherman for 140 years!

More realistic is the headstone of 113 year old Ralph Bourn set into the church wall at West Tanfield (99: SE 268/788). The shortest person was Jane Ridsdale who was only 31' high and is commemorated in the south aisle of St Thomas Beckets at Hampsthwaite (104: SE 259/591).

The Sanctuary Seat in Beverley Minster.

14 England's Largest Parish Church

Position: Beverley (N Humberside)
O.S. Map: Kingston upon Hull & surrounding area: Sheet No. 107
Map Ref: TA 044/394
Access: Beverley is about 7 miles north-west of Kingston upon Hull on the A1079 and A1174 and the Minster is signposted.

Beverley's Gothic Minster Church of St John the Evangelist is the biggest parish church in England. The original church dated from the late seventh-century but the present structure was built over three centuries from about 1230.

One of its curiosities is the Sanctuary Chair (or Frith Stool) which is a thousand years old and may have been used by the Saintly John of Beverley. If anyone sought sanctuary in the church and was prepared to give all they had in the way of property to the Crown and to dedicate themselves to the Church, they could remain freely in Beverley instead of facing trial.

Also in the Minster is a very rare 14th century man-powered treadmill used to raise building materials to the roof, which still works. It is concealed in the roof and can be seen by appointment.

Not to be missed is a group of 68 stalls with superb misericords depicting heraldry, mythology and everyday life, forming the largest such group in England. A misericord is a carved wooden projection underneath a hinged seat which offered support to the parishioner when the seat was raised.

St Mary's Church in Beverley is famous for its Minstrels' Pillar depicting 5 minstrels with their musical instruments. Over one of the doorways is a carved hare with a shoulder bag which may have inspired the character of the March Hare to Lewis Carroll, who attended service when staying with friends.

Also in Beverley are some mock-Tudor houses near North Bar built at the end of the nineteenth-century and decorated with carved cartoons from *'Punch'* magazine!

Places of Interest in the Neighbourhood
8. Monument to the Slave Emancipator
9. Yorkshire's Last Complete Windmill

√15 Bettison's Dinner Time Tower

Position: Hornsea (N Humberside)
O.S. Map: Kingston upon Hull & surrounding area: Sheet No. 107
Map Ref: TA 205/476
Access: Hornsea is on the east coast 12 miles north-east of Beverley on the B1244 and the Tower is on Willows Drive opposite the museum.

Bettison's Folly is a 50 feet high, round brick-built tower with mock castellations at the top. It was erected by a Mr W Bettison in 1844 to serve as a carriage-watching tower. His servants were expected to climb the tower in order to catch sight of their master's carriage returning home. They would then pass the word on to the kitchen staff at the house who would thus be able to prepare dinner in good time for his arrival!

Wassand Hall at Seaton (TA 174/463) 2½ miles west of Hornsea on the B1244 is a brick villa built by Thomas Cundy in 1812. Its most curious feature is the circular Mushroom Cottage on the side of the Hornsea road. It has pointed Gothic windows and rustic wooden pillars which once supported a thatched roof.

Finally, 10 miles south of Hornsea off the B1242 is Grimston Garth (TA 283/352). This is a Gothic triangular house built in the 1780's by John Carr for Thomas Grimston, during a period when triangular buildings were fashionable. It consists of a tall hexagonal tower containing a Gothic and a Chinese room. This is surrounded by a castellated triangle of 3 smaller towers. The surrounding buildings and stables also have mock castellations, and the gatehouse added 30 years later even boasts a portcullis!

Places of Interest in the Neighbourhood
No other sites lie within a 10 miles radius of Hornsea.

Mr Bettison's carriage-watching tower at Hornsea.

31

√16 Humberside's Temple of the Winds

Position: Carnaby (N Humberside)
O.S. Map: Scarborough & Bridlington area: Sheet No. 101
Map Ref: TA 142/666
Access: Carnaby is 2½ miles south-west of Bridlington on the A166
and the temple is 3/4 mile north-west along Temple Lane.

Carnaby Temple is one of Humberside's few great follies. It was built
by Sir George Strickland of nearby Boynton Hall (see No. 18) in 1770
and is an interpretation of the famous Temple of the Winds which
still stands today in the Roman 'Agora' (market place) in Athens.
Octagonal in plan and constructed in brick, it is two storeys high with a
domed roof topped by an octagonal lantern. Although its arched
windows have now been blocked up to prevent vandalism it is still a
grand structure set as it is amidst open fields stretching towards the sea.

Places of Interest in the Neighbourhood
17. Several Shining Examples
18. The Turkey Lectern
19. Britain's Tallest Bronze Age Monument
23. Lock, Stock and Barrel!

The Temple of the Winds at Carnaby.

17 Several Shining Examples

Position: Flamborough (N Humberside)
O.S. Map: Scarborough & Bridlington area: Sheet No. 101
Map Ref: TA 250/708
Access: Flamborough is 3 miles north-east of Bridlington on the B1255
and its lighthouses are on Flamborough Head further along the B1259.

The green fields of Flamborough come to a dramatic halt at Flamborough Head, where jagged 170 feet high chalk headlands jut out into
the North Sea. Like much of the Yorkshire coast, this is a very
dangerous area for shipping and the county's oldest lighthouse was
built here in 1674 by Sir John Clayton (see frontispiece). It is an
octagonal 4-storey tower built of chalk and is the only intact coal light
in England. A new lighthouse was built closer to the sea in 1806 with a
signal comprising 4 white flares. In 1859 a fog cannon was installed,
then rockets in 1877, a horn in 1913 and radio bleeps in 1985. Its light is
said to be visible 21 miles away.

Further down the coast is Spurn Head (113: TA 404/113), the tip of
a 3 ½ mile long spit of land created by the continual deposition of
material eroded by the sea from further up the coast. It is a precarious,
storm battered place where the sea is constantly altering the coastline.
The present lighthouse was built in 1895 and is 120 feet high, replacing
an earlier one of 1776, and another dating to 1852. As the coast moves
so does the position of the lighthouse!

Finally at Paull (113: TA 173/250), an old-time fishing village overlooking the Humber estuary, there is a quaint lighthouse built in 1836
now used as a private dwelling.

Places of Interest in the Neighbourhood
16. Humberside's Temple of the Winds
18. The Turkey Lectern
19. Britain's Tallest Bronze Age Monument

18 The Turkey Lectern

Position: Boynton (N Humberside)
O.S. Map: Scarborough & Bridlington area: Sheet No. 101
Map Ref: TA 136/680
Access: Boynton is 3 miles north-west of Bridlington on the B1253.

St Andrew's Church at Boynton houses several monuments to the
locally famous Strickland family of nearby Boynton Hall. These include
2 black and gold columned tablets to William Strickland (d. 1673) and
Elizabeth Strickland (d. 1674) as well as sarcophagi and obelisks to Sir
William Strickland. However, the most curious must surely be the brass
lectern in the shape of a turkey, commemorating the introduction of the

The Turkey Lectern in Boynton Church.

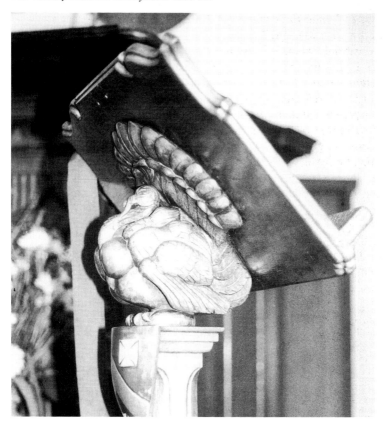

bird into England by Sir William Strickland.

Boynton Hall itself (TA 139/678), ¼ mile south-east of the church, was built by an earlier William Strickland who died in 1598. It has an interesting but complex architectural history involving numerous styles and materials. Inside can be found a glorious carved staircase (1700) and large chimneybreasts in the Oak Room and Drawing Room (c.1730).

Another Strickland family venture was the striking Carnaby Temple (see No. 16) just outside Bridlington, built in 1770 for Sir George Strickland.

Places of Interest in the Neighbourhood
16. Humberside's Temple of the Winds
17. Several Shining Examples
19. Britain's Tallest Bronze Age Monument
23. Lock, Stock and Barrel!

The Monolith in the churchyard at Rudston.

19 Britain's Tallest Bronze Age Monument

Position: Rudston (N Humberside)
O.S. Map: Scarborough & Bridlington area: Sheet No. 101
Map Ref: TA 098/678
Access: Rudston is 5 miles west of Bridlington on the B1253 and the monolith is in All Saints churchyard.

The monolith at Rudston is 25 feet 6 inches in height with a circumference of 6 feet and is thought to have been standing for some 4000 years. It may once have been even taller as its top is damaged and protected by a metal cap. It is formed of gritstone and probably comes from Cayton or Cornelian Bay 10 miles to the north. Erected as some sort of ceremonial marker stone, local legend says that the Devil threw it at the church but missed! There is a smaller gritstone in the cemetery as well as a slab-built cist grave, which together with the nearby earthen ditches and mounds visible from the air, show the Rudston area to have been an important Neolithic and Bronze Age ritual site.

Also in the churchyard is the grave of Winifred Holtby, the famous Yorkshire novelist who wrote *The Land of Green Ginger* and *South Riding*. She was born in Rudston and died in 1935 at the early age of 37.

Nearby Wold Newton (TA 038/721) also boasts an obelisk, but this time marking the place where a meteorite landed in 1795. It was dug up and placed in London's Geological Museum.

Places of Interest in the Neighbourhood
16. Humberside's Temple of the Winds
17. Several Shining Examples
18. The Turkey Lectern
23. Lock, Stock and Barrel!

20 A Family of Folly Builders

Position: Sledmere (N Humberside)
O.S. Map: Scarborough & Bridlington area: Sheet No. 101
Map Ref: SE 93/64
Access: Sledmere is 8 miles north-west of Driffield on the B1252 and the
House and grounds are open to the public from April 30th to 1st
October (except Mondays and Fridays).

Sledmere House (SE 932/647) has always been home to the famous
Sykes family, originally Leeds merchants, who were responsible for 150
years of folly-building up until the end of the Great War.

The first folly builder was Sir Christopher Sykes, a great agricultural
innovator, who 'made the Wolds' barren waste fertile'. He built Sledmere Castle (SE 949/645) from a design by John Carr as an eyecatcher
for the great house and its enclosed park, the latter undertaken by
Lancelot 'Capability' Brown in the 1770's. The castle was intended to
resemble a castellated gatehouse which would mask a farm behind it.
Another eyecatcher of the same period is an arch on a hilltop near the
B1251 to the south-west.

Long after Christopher's death in 1801 the village well at the park
entrance was embellished with a Tuscan rotunda as his memorial by Sir
Tatton Sykes, a stockbreeder and sportsman.

It was the son of the latter, another Sir Tatton (1826-1913), who
inherited the estate in 1863 and became the family's true eccentric. Soon
after his mother's death he ripped up all the lawns and flowers in the
village because his mother so loved them! He also forbade his tenants to
build front doors in new houses insisting they must be false ones only!
He did, however, spend two million pounds restoring East Riding
churches and in 1865 he built the Sir Tatton Sykes monument on
Garton Hill, 3 miles south-east of the house on the B1252 (SE 957/618).
It is a 120 feet high tapering four-sided Gothic tower with carved panels
around the base, one showing old Sir Tatton on horseback. It is
inscribed '... to the memory of Sir Tatton Sykes, Baronet, by those who
loved him as a friend and honoured as a landlord.' The younger Sir
Tatton erected his own memorial in 1895 (the Eleanor Cross) in the
village, a copy of Northampton Cross (1291) depicting carvings of
saints which was later converted to a First World War memorial.

Finally came the Waggoners' Memorial, a chunky column designed
by the next heir, Lt. Col. Mark Sykes. It commemorates his Waggoners
Special Reserve, a group of Yorkshire Wolds farmers with equine skills

who provided the transport for the Expeditionary Force to France, the first group of civilians involved in the Great War. It was Sir Mark, a soldier, politician and traveller, who built the tile-lined Turkish room in Sledmere House, based on a mosque in Istanbul.

Places of Interest in the Neighbourhood
19. Britain's Tallest Bronze Age Monument
21. A Lost Medieval Village

Sledmere Castle - an eyecatcher for Sledmere House.

21 A Lost Medieval Village

Position: Wharram Percy (N Yorks)
O.S. Map: Malton, Pickering & surrounding area: Sheet No. 100
Map Ref: SE 859/645
Access: Wharram Percy is 6 miles south-east of Malton on a minor
road off the B1248, ½ a mile south of Wharram-le-Street. It is an
English Heritage property open all year round.

There are hundreds of deserted villages in England, and North
Yorkshire is no exception, indeed one in six of villages in the Yorkshire
Wolds are now deserted. However, Wharram Percy is unusual in that it
has been carefully excavated by the Medieval Village Research Group
and provides us with a valuable picture of rural life from the
Anglo-Saxon period up to the sixteenth-century. The word 'Wharram'
derives from the Scandinavian for 'at the bends', whilst the Percys were
the medieval lords of the manor.

Among the numerous reasons for the desertion of villages is a climatic
deterioration in the thirteenth-century, the ravages of war, eviction by
Cistercian monks who were creating monastic estates, and, in 1348, the
effect of the Black Death. Following this many landlords abandoned
arable farming and began large-scale sheep farming, and this may have
been the reason for the desertion of Wharram Percy.

Today only ground plans of the village houses can be detected, and
little reaches above ground level. However, its church continued in use
long after the village had disintegrated. St Mary's contains Saxon and
Norman fragments but was at its largest in the thirteenth and four-
teenth-centuries. The chancel was rebuilt in the seventeenth-century
and the aisles destroyed, after which the church shrank visibly. Services
continued for the local people of Thixendale until 1870, when they built
their own church, and occasional services occurred until the 1940's. The
church is now roofless and forlorn.

Places of Interest in the Neighbourhood
13. Grave Concerns!
20. A Family of Folly Builders
22. England's Largest Folly

A ruined church in the deserted village of Wharram Percy.

22 England's Largest Folly

Position: Castle Howard (N Yorks)
O.S. Map: Malton, Pickering & surrounding area: Sheet No. 100
Map Ref: SE 71/69
Access: Castle Howard is 5 miles south-west of Malton off the A64 and is open daily between March 25th and November 1st.

People visit Castle Howard for a variety of reasons, including the sheer grandeur of its buildings and landscaped gardens and the fact that the television version of Evelyn Waugh's *Brideshead Revisited* was filmed here. However, for the visitor interested in curiosities it is the enclosing ramparts which stretch around the estate that are of interest. Their tremendous length, of some 2,000 feet, and 11 towers, make it Britain's largest folly as well as the first sham fortification for display not defence. One of the gates was by Nicholas Hawksmoor and another by Sir John Vanbrugh with its flanking pavilions and pyramidal roof.

Other curious edifices in the grounds include Hawksmoor's Pyramid (SE 719/692), a magnificent Mausoleum (SE 727/696) and 100 feet high obelisk (SE 708/699), as well as Vanbrugh's fine Temple of the Four Winds (SE 723/699). The fountain is unusual in depicting Atlas holding aloft a globe decorated with the signs of the Zodiac. The globe was bought by the Howard family at the 1889 Paris Great Exhibition.

The main building at Castle Howard was commissioned by Charles Howard, 3rd Earl of Carlisle, firstly from Talman but following a dispute from Vanbrugh and was built between 1699 and 1726.

Places of Interest in the Neighbourhood
21. A Lost Medieval Village
42. Amazing Mazes

23 Lock, Stock and Barrel!

Position: Hunmanby (N Yorks)
O.S. Map: Scarborough & Bridlington area: Sheet No. 101
Map Ref: SE 095/775
Access: Hunmanby is 2½ miles south-west of Filey off the A165 and
the lock-up is situated on the village green.

At Hunmanby there is a two-celled village lock-up made more curious
by the fact that it is positioned next door to a circular stone pound (or
pinfold). The former with its roof and barred windows held miscreants
who strayed from the straight and narrow, whereas the latter held stray
sheep and cattle until recovered by their owners. It was run by the
pinman or pinder.

   Another fine pinfold is the elaborate brick-built one at Raskelf (100:
SE 493/710) 2½ miles north-west of Easingwold off the A19. It
has an arched door and windows and battlements along the top.
Other pinfolds can be seen at Appleton-le-Moors (100: SE 735/878),
Birstwith (104: SE 239/596), Buckden (98: SD 943/772), Carperby (98:
SE 007/897), Dringhouses (105: SE 588/497), East Witton (99: SE

The lock-up and pinfold at Hunmanby.

145/860), Follifoot (104: SE 343/525), Hutton Buscel (101: SE 973/841), Hutton-le-Hole (100: SE 706/899), Mickley (99: SE 255/770), Redmire (98: SE 045/913), Spennithorne (99: SE 138/889), Spofforth (104: SE 363/510), Stokesley (93: NZ 526/086), and Threshfield (98: SD 989/636).

Of relevance here are those instruments of punishment from yesteryear, the village stocks. A good example is in Ripley where miscreants sat on the lowest step of the village cross with their legs in the stocks (see no. 80). Other examples are at Malham (98: SD 903/629), Ripon (99: SE 315/713), West Burton (98: SE 017/867) and Skipton (103: SD 993/519).

Returning to Hunmanby there is a folly in the form of a sham ruined archway erected by Squire Humphrey Osbaldeston early in the nineteenth-century.

Places of Interest in the Neighbourhood
16. Humberside's Temple of the Winds
18. The Turkey Lectern
19. Britain's Tallest Bronze Age Monument
25. Some Curious Yorkshire Churches
27. Scarborough's Skipping Custom

A miniature hall outside the village of Ebberston.

24 A King's Cave and a Miniature Mansion

Position: Ebberston (N Yorks)
O.S. Map: Scarborough & Bridlington area: Sheet No. 101
Map Ref: See below
Access: The village of Ebberston is on the A170 Pickering road 9 ½ miles south-west of Scarborough. Ebberston Hall is open to the public from Easter to October 1st.

On the moors to the north above the villages of Ebberston and Allerston can be found Bloody Field and Alfred's Cave. Legend associates both sites with the seventh-century Battle of Ebberston in which King Aldfrith of Northumbria fought his father King Oswy. Aldfrith was stabbed and took shelter in a cave on a rocky crag overlooking Ebberston (SE 895/849) which was known thereafter as Alfred's Cave. Whether he died here or not is unknown, but in 1790 a sham tumulus was erected as a memorial. The battle could well have taken place amongst the nearby prehistoric earthworks known as Scamridge Dykes (SE 89/85), now somewhat ironically a picturesque picnic site and viewpoint.

Ebberston Hall lies in the wooded Kirk Dale just to the west of the village (SE 893/834). Built in the Palladian style in 1718 it is more a tiny and elegant summer villa than a full-blown mansion. It was designed for William Thompson M.P. by Colin Campbell, a distinguished Scottish architect who later became architect to the Prince of Wales. Only one storey high it comprises a large columned doorway leading to a short corridor which runs straight to the back door. Off the corridor are the rooms decorated elaborately with wood and plaster in the Ionic and Corinthian style. A chief feature of the house was its water garden to the rear with a 1,200 feet long Italian-style canal and cascade, but sadly little remains to be seen.

Places of Interest in the Neighbourhood

25 Some Curious Yorkshire Churches

Position: Wykeham (N Yorks)
O.S. Map: Scarborough & Bridlington area: Sheet No. 101
Map Ref: SE 965/853
Access: The village of Wykeham is 6 miles south-west of Scarborough on the A170.

Most of Yorkshire's churches can boast a long and interesting history as well as a curiosity or two. Several have been discussed elsewhere (see nos. 1, 10, 14, 18, 34, 50, 60, 71, 76) but below are a few more of our favourites.

All Saints at Wykeham was built in 1853 but its churchyard entrance ('lych-gate') is formed by a curious tower which is all that remains of the fourteenth-century chapel of St Mary and St Helen.

In St Wilfred's at South Kilvington (99: SE 426/840) a mile north of Thirsk is an old hourglass near the pulpit used to time the length of the sermon. Some of the woodwork here is by William Towler Kingsley, cousin of author Charles Kingsley, and England's oldest parson who spent the last 58 of his 101 years as rector here until his death in 1917! An hourglass can also be seen in St Nicholas' at Keyingham (107: TA 245/255) 10 miles south-east of Hull, and at Croft-on-Tees (93: NZ 288/098) 3 miles south of Darlington.

St Gregory's at Bedale (99: SE 265/884) 7 ½ miles south-west of Nor-thallerton has a unique early fourteenth-century fortified church tower said to have been built as a place of refuge from Border raiders. The stairs to the first floor once had a portcullis. Other fortified churches are at Middleham (99: SE 127/878) south-east of Leyburn and Melsonby (92: NZ 198/083) north-east of Richmond.

All Saints at Easingwold (100: SE 526/701) 13 miles north-west of York contains an unusual old parish coffin for common use. In the churchyard of St Robert's at Pannal (105: SE 307/518) 2 miles south of Harrogate is a 'mortsafe', a heavy stone slab placed over new graves to prevent bodysnatchers removing new corpses to sell to surgeons, a prac-tice prohibited by Act of Parliament in 1832.

In St Peter and St Paul's at Pickering (100: SE 799/840) 11 miles north of Malton is a series of mid fifteenth-century wall paintings re-discovered in 1851, one of which depicts Herod's feast in all its details.

Finally at Raskelf (100: SE 490/708) 3 miles west of Easingwold is a unique late fifteenth-century timber church tower, whilst All Saints at Weston (104: SE 178/467) 2 miles north-west of Otley contains a squire's 'parlour' complete with fireplace.

Places of Interest in the Neighbourhood
23. Lock, Stock and Barrel!
24. A King's Cave and a Miniature Mansion
26. A Magnificent Man and his Flying Machine
27. Scarborough's Skipping Custom

The curious 'lych-gate' to All Saints at Wykeham.

26 A Magnificent Man and his Flying Machine

Position: Ayton (N Yorks)
O.S. Map: Scarborough & Bridlington area: Sheet No. 101
Map Ref: SE 993/850
Access: Ayton lies 4 miles south-west of Scarborough on the A170 and Brompton is 3 miles further on.

Everyone knows that the Wright brothers were the pioneers of powered flight, but it was a Yorkshire man who first actually built a winged structure which flew, albeit without an engine.

Sir George Cayley (1773-1853) was a man of many talents; an inventor, writer and scientist. He was interested in railway engineering and allotments, was inventor of a new type of telescope, artificial limbs and the caterpillar tractor, and initiated the science of aerodynamics which pushed forward the possibility of flight. His first model glider was built in 1804 and a fullsize example followed in 1809. However, it was in 1853 at Brompton Dale (SE: 937/833), north of Brompton, that he pioneered manned flight. His coachman flew a glider 50 yards, although after his short but significant flight the pilot resigned on the grounds that his terms of employment did not include flying!

A porch was added to All Saints Church at Brompton as a memorial to Cayley – 'The Father of Aeronautics'. It was also here on October 4th 1802 that William Wordsworth married locally born Mary Hutchinson.

Places of Interest in the Neighbourhood
23. Lock, Stock and Barrel!
24. A King's Cave and a Miniature Mansion
25. Some Curious Yorkshire Churches
27. Scarborough's Skipping Custom

27 Scarborough's Skipping Custom

Position: Scarborough (N Yorks)
O.S Map: Scarborough & Bridlington area: Sheet No. 101
Map Ref: TA 045/882
Access: Scarborough is on the east coast of Yorkshire 15 miles east of
Pickering on the A170.

Scarborough is England's oldest holiday resort, but its earlier fame
from 1698 was as a spa. It has many curiosities. In the Rotunda
Museum, near the junction of Valley and Foreshore Roads in the South
Bay, hangs a bell known as the Pancake Bell. It originally hung in the
old St Thomas's Hospital, now demolished, when it was used to sound
the curfew. However, as the Pancake Bell, it is rung at noon on Shrove

The Rotunda Museum and Grand Hotel at Scarborough.

Tuesdays and signals time for housewives to make pancakes. Pancakes were traditionally a convenient, and tasty, way of using up eggs before the period of Lenten abstinence.

The bell also signals another custom for which Scarborough is famous. Since at least 1903, on hearing the bell, many of the good townsfolk go down to the foreshore and skip, in small or large groups, accompanied by rhymes similar to those sung by children in the street. Skipping is thought by some to be an ancient and magical activity which occurred on such places as burial mounds and was supposed to stimulate crop growth. One theory why it occurs on Shrove Tuesday is that at that time of year the fishermen sort out their lines as they finish line fishing and set pots instead. There would thus be plenty of odd pieces of rope around and the skipping would soon produce an appetite for pancakes!

Places of Interest in the Neighbourhood
23. Lock, Stock and Barrel!
24. A King's Cave and a Miniature Mansion
25. Some Curious Yorkshire Churches
26. A Magnificent Man and his Flying Machine

28 Always a Warm Welcome

Position: Saltergate (N Yorks)
O.S Map: Whitby & surrounding area: Sheet No. 94
Map Ref: SE 853/944
Access: The Saltergate Inn is on the A169 Whitby road 8 ½ miles
north-east of Pickering.

The Saltergate Inn was built in 1648 and contains a peat fire which has
reputedly burned continuously since 1801. Some say that the victim
of a fight between smugglers and customs officers lies buried below
the hearth. Others tell of a local hermit who told the landlord that
the building would be destroyed if the fire went out! Once a stopping
place for stagecoaches and a tollhouse, it was called The Saltergate Inn
because it lay on the Robin Hood's Bay road, whence fish was brought
for salting before being sent to towns inland.

Other Yorkshire pubs of interest include the Busby Stoop Inn (99: SE
383/808) 3 miles west of Thirsk at the junction of the A167 and A61,
named after a man hanged here in 1702 for clipping coins. His favourite
chair at the inn has had to be stored away after tragedy befell two
customers who used his chair after his death. Another story tells of a
Tom Busby hanged for killing his father-in-law over money and how his
stooping ghost haunts the inn in search of his chair.

There are more inns standing over 1,000 feet in Yorkshire than any-
where else. The Tan Hill Inn (92: NY 896/068) 4 ½ miles north of Keld
near Arkengarthdale is the highest in Britain at 1,732 feet and was
much used by the lead and coal mining communities.

The Cat and Bagpipes Inn at East Harsley (99: SE 422/996) 5 miles
north-east of Northallerton is named after the Scottish cross-border
raiders known as 'caterans' who were once active here. It also reflects
the Scottish drovers who passed this way taking their cattle to market.

Places of Interest in the Neighbourhood
24. A King's Cave and a Miniature Mansion
29. Of Romans and Giants
30. The Railway across the Moors
32. Eccentric Animal Houses
33. A Smugglers' Cove

29 Of Romans and Giants

Position: Wheeldale Moor (N Yorks)
O.S. Map: Whitby & surrounding area: Sheet No. 94
Map Ref: SE 803/973
Access: 'Wade's Causeway' Roman road runs north-east from
Cawthorn to the River Esk at Grosmont crossing Wheeldale Moor.
Here there is a mile-long preserved section (Dept. of Environment)
which is 8 miles north of Pickering via Newton-on-Rawcliffe and Stape,
where there is parking.

Of the numerous Roman remains in Yorkshire one of the most unusual is the road known as 'Wade's Causeway', which is regarded as
one of the best preserved Roman roads in Britain. It is of characteristic construction being some 16 feet wide and comprising a low rubble
foundation (or 'agger') lined with drains down either side. Originally it
would have been paved with stone slabs and covered with gravel. The
road leads north from the Roman camp at Cawthorn (SE 785/901) and
is thought to have been built in about 100 A.D. to connect Malton with
a series of Roman camps and signal stations on the Yorkshire coast. An
example is in the grounds of the Castle on the headland at Scarborough,
(101: TA 050/893) an English Heritage site open all year.

Local legend gives us a different story in the form of the giant Wade
and his wife Bell. Along with their giant child they are said to have lived
at Foss Castle in the grounds of Mulgrave Castle (NZ 839/117) near
Sandsend, where a whale's jawbone could once be seen, said to be the
rib from Bell's giant cow! It was in order to assist Bell in her daily
walk to Pickering Castle to milk her cows that Wade constructed the
causeway for her. Many of the hugh stones and hillocks visible from the
road are said to have been the surplus material tossed aside during
construction. Wade's grave is at Goldsborough (NZ 831/129) where
two great stones a hundred feet apart straddle the A174.

Places of Interest in the Neighbourhood
28. Always a Warm Welcome!
30. The Railway across the Moors
31. The Planting of the Penny Hedge
32. Eccentric Animal Houses
37. The Beggars Bridge

The 'Wade's Causeway' Roman road across Wheeldale Moor.

30 The Railway across the Moors

Position: Beck Hole (N Yorks)
O.S. Map: Whitby & surrounding area: Sheet No. 94
Map Ref: SE 823/022
Access: Beck Hole is in the Esk Valley 8 miles south-west of Whitby off
the A169, north of Goathland, and the old railway station and incline
are at the end of a footpath opposite the pub.

One of the longest privately operated railways in Britain is the North
Yorkshire Moors Railway, otherwise known as Moorsrail. It runs
steam locomotives and a diesel railcar between Pickering in the south
and Grosmont in the north where it joins up with the British Rail
Middlesbrough to Whitby line. It is a picturesque ride with stops at
Goathland and Levisham.

George Stephenson originated the line in 1836 using stage coaches on
bogies drawn by horses along the track. This ran from Grosmont to
Goathland via Beck Hole where the gradient was between 1 in 15 and 1
in 10. This incline necessitated the wagons being hauled uphill by rope,
which was wound on a 10 feet wide drum.

Steam was introduced to the line in 1845 by George Hudson 'the
Railway King' but the incline still caused trouble. Finally, in 1865 the
incline was circumvented by the blasting through of the present Devia-
tion Line. The incline was still used occasionally for special purposes
such as the testing of an engine to be used in Brazil and for an autocar
tourist service used until 1914.

The line was eventually closed as part of the Beeching cuts, but
fortunately the newly formed North Yorkshire Moors Railway Preser-
vation Society bought the line from Grosmont to Ellerbeck and it
reopened in 1973. Today 3 ½ miles of Stephenson's original route can
be followed as an Historic Railway Trail from Grosmont to Goathland,
where one of Stephenson's original rail ties can be seen.

Places of Interest in the Neighbourhood
28. Always a Warm Welcome!
29. Of Romans and Giants
31. The Planting of the Penny Hedge
32. Eccentric Animal Houses
37. The Beggars Bridge

31 The Planting of the Penny Hedge

Position: Sleights (N Yorks)
O.S. Map: Whitby & surrounding area: Sheet No. 94
Map Ref: NZ 860/072
Access: Sleights is in Eskdale 3 ½ miles south-west of Whitby on the
A169 and the chapel lies 1 ½ miles upstream close to the railway.

At 9 a.m. on the eve of Ascension Day (50 days after Easter) on the
east side of Whitby's Upper Harbour near Boyes' Staith there takes
place the odd custom of planting the Penny Hedge. Its origin finds
some explanation in a local legend which runs as follows. In 1159 two
lords and a gentleman met to hunt wild boar on land belonging to the
Abbot of Whitby. While in hot pursuit one such boar hid and died in a
hermitage belonging to one of the abbey's monks. The now ruinous
chapel can still be seen today. The monk continued his prayers until the
hunters arrived but on finding the boar dead they killed the monk in
frustration. As he lay dying the monk graciously forgave the hunters
and permitted them to continue using the estate for hunting so long as
they observed the custom of the Penny (or Penance) Hedge. This necessitated them cutting a number of stakes from a specified wood and
carrying them to Whitby. Here they were to erect a woven fence or
hedge in the harbour mud which would withstand three tides whilst also
calling out for repentance.

Today the legend is thought to be fictitious. However the custom does
seem to have roots in the much older Horngarth Service, itself an
ancient tenure custom. Numerous explanations have been put forward
for the derivation of the word 'Horngarth' and for the nature of its
attendant service, which stretches back to the founding of Whitby
Abbey in AD657 and beyond. It would seem to have been some sort of
communal boundary which tenants had to help maintain, possibly to
contain wild deer. The 'horn' refers either to the musical instrument
which now accompanies the hedge planting or else it is the type of stick
used. The 'garth' refers to the fence.

On Sleights Lane End at the junction of the A171 and A169 is a
plaque marking where the first enemy aircraft to be shot down in
England in the Second World War crashed. It occurred on 3rd February
1940 and the British pilot responsible was Peter Townsend, known for
his romance with HRH the Princess Margaret.

(No. 31 continued)

Places of Interest in the Neighbourhood

The magnificent classical pigsty at Fylingthorpe.

32 Eccentric Animal Houses

Position: Fylingthorpe (N Yorks)
O.S. Map: Whitby & surrounding area: Sheet No. 94
Map Ref: SE 936/041
Access: Fylingthorpe is 4½ miles southeast of Whitby off the A171 and the pigsty is in the grounds of Fyling Old Hall at the bend, south of Fyling Hall School.

The pigsty at Fyling Old Hall is one of the most magnificent examples of animal architecture in Britain. Its facade resembles an Ionic Greek Temple with a pediment atop a columned portico. It is supported on a base of local stone brought on a horse-drawn sledge from a nearby quarry. The building took three men two years to complete, since the eccentric Squire Barry for whom it was built kept altering his designs. It dates to c. 1883 but was recently subject to complete restoration by The Landmark Trust who have converted it into one of their unusual holiday properties for rent. A fullsize stone statue of a pig in one of the rooms reminds guests of the original purpose of the building!

A different creature altogether was housed in Bedale (99: SE 268/883) just off the A1 on the A684 Wensleydale road. Here on the bank of the river next to the bridge is a leech house, a small brick building with pointed windows and battlements used to breed leeches for use in early medicinal practice.

Places of Interest in the Neighbourhood
30. The Railway across the Moors
31. The Planting of the Penny Hedge
33. A Smugglers' Cove
34. The Home of England's First Poet
35. A Museumful of Curiosities!

33 A Smugglers' Cove

Position: Robin Hood's Bay (N Yorks)
O.S. Map: Whitby & surrounding area: Sheet No. 94
Map Ref: SE 953/049
Access: Robin Hood's Bay is on the Yorkshire coast 5 miles south-east of Whitby on the A171/B1447.

Many a curious story of the sea can be relived at the quaint and picturesque village of Robin Hood's Bay. Firstly why Robin Hood's Bay? It was only called that from the reign of Henry VIII onwards, but what was Robin Hood doing so far north of his native Sherwood? Stories abound, one of which claims he was hounded out of Nottingham and found refuge on the North Yorkshire moors. Whatever the reason, references to him are numerous, including Little John's House on New Road and Sherwood Cottage on the corner of King Street. However, 'Robin Hood's Butts' (SE 956/022) where he and his men could be presumed to have practised their archery, are in fact Bronze Age burial mounds!

If these stories are apocryphal, there is no doubting the evidence that smuggling was once rife here. The Old Mariners, once an inn, is a house on The Square which in former times was frequented by smugglers and may have a tunnel leading to the cliffs. Look out for the old insurance plaque on the wall. The Fisherman's Arms in the Dock area has smugglers' tunnels to other houses nearby, though they are now blocked.

The streets are so steep and the houses' staircases so winding that a local curiosity is the coffin window at landing level to facilitate easy removal of coffins (e.g. Littlewood Cottage in Fisherhead).

A 'Coffin Window' at Robin Hood's Bay.

34 The Home of England's First Poet

Position: Whitby (N Yorks)
O.S. Map: Whitby & surrounding area: Sheet No. 94
Map Ref: NZ 904/113
Access: Whitby is on the Yorkshire coast 18½ miles north-east of
Pickering on the A169. The Abbey is on the cliff top east of the town
centre and is an English Heritage property open all year.

Whitby's Abbey must occupy one of the most spectacular of positions,
perched as it is on a high, wind-swept headland overlooking the estuary
and town below. It is built on the site of an Anglo-Saxon monastery
founded in 657. A Northumbrian princess, St Hilda, was its first Abbess
– the admittance of both men and women was a feature of the Anglo-
Saxon Church. Its story is told by the Venerable Bede who relates that

Whitby Harbour, overlooked by the Abbey and Church.

Caedmon, England's first poet, lived and worked here. In 664 the Synod of Whitby was held here which upheld the supremacy of Rome over the Celtic Church and also fixed the date of Easter.

The Abbey was refounded as a Benedictine monastery towards the end of the eleventh-century. Its exposed location made it vulnerable to piratical raids and damage was even sustained during German naval bombardment in the Great War. The ruins seen today include excavated monastic cells and the two remaining facades from the thirteenth-century.

Next to the Abbey is St Mary's Church. Its graveyard runs to the edge of the cliff and contains several weathered headstones to drowned sailors and lifeboatmen. Bram Stoker is said to have used this atmospheric place as a setting for his Gothic tale *Dracula*. However, the church interior, remodelled in the eighteenth-century, is the real curiosity since it escaped alteration by the High Church movement in the nineteenth-century. As such its interior, which resembles a ship, retains its superb Georgian arrangement of galleries, box-pews and 3-decker pulpit. The largest pew is for the Cholmleys (c.1600), the lords of the Manor, and there is a large stove in the nave. Another curiosity is the system of voice tubes emanating from the pulpit to amplify the parson's sermons.

The headland can be reached by a flight of 199 steps leading up from the town. Called the Donkey Steps, there is a steep path alongside up which a man once drove his coach and horses. A large cross at the top commemorates the poet Caedmon.

Places of Interest in the Neighbourhood
30. The Railway across the Moors
31. The Planting of the Penny Hedge
32. Eccentric Animal Houses
33. A Smugglers' Cove
35. A Museumful of Curiosities

35 A Museumful of Curiosities!

Position: Whitby (N Yorks)
O.S. Map: Whitby & surrounding area: Sheet No. 94
Map Ref: NZ 892/108
Access: Whitby is on the Yorkshire coast 18½ miles north-east of
Pickering on the A169. Whitby Museum is on the West Cliff in Pannett
Park, off St Hilda's Terrace, and is open all year round.

The Museum at Whitby was founded by the local Literary and
Philosophical Society in 1823 in rooms over two shops in Baxtergate. It
has occupied its present site in Pannett Park since 1931, where it stands
witness to the great interest in local history which Whitby has indulged
in for over 150 years.

    Although the museum building is not particularly old nor of great

Fossilized ichthyosaurs set in the walls of Whitby Museum.

architectural interest, within is a different world. Here Victorian false teeth, Anglo-Saxon combs from the nearby Abbey and whalers' harpoons jostle for space in row-upon-row of glass fronted cabinets - a wondrously old fashioned museum!

Amongst its many important collections the observant visitor will discover an array of curiosities. A favourite is the model of the eccentrically named 'Tempest Prognosticator', a barometer worked by 12 bottled leeches whose writhings worked 12 metal clappers forecasting the weather.

A local curiosity is the grisly 'Hand of Glory' last used in Eskdale in 1820. This was a hand cut from a dead body hanging on the gibbet, preserved and baked hard. It was carried as a talisman by burglars, together with a candle made of fat from the corpse, and was said to hypnotize the burglars' victims. The spell could only be broken by extinguishing the candle with blood or milk.

The type of 'coal' known as Jet can be found on the shore and has been carved locally since prehistoric times. In the Victorian period it became an industry employing a tenth of the population, and exhibited is a beautifully carved card tray which won the 1886 Jet Exhibition.

Whitby has long been a great fishing port and for a period saw much whaling traffic. Its leading lights were the Scoresbys, one of whom invented the crows nest. Another was a great captain and Arctic whaler who became Vicar of Bradford, and on display are his maps and intricate drawings of snowflakes. On the nearby headland can be seen an archway made up of the ribs of a great whale.

Of course Captain Cook has a gallery to himself as he lived in Whitby before embarking on his voyages (see no. 36).

Places of Interest in the Neighbourhood
30. The Railway across the Moors
31. The Planting of the Penny Hedge
32. Eccentric Animal Houses
33. A Smugglers' Cove
34. The Home of England's First Poet

36 In the Footsteps of Captain Cook

Position: Staithes (N Yorks)
O.S. Map: Whitby & surrounding area: Sheet No. 94
Map Ref: NZ 784/188
Access: The village of Staithes is on the Yorkshire coast 9 miles north-west of Whitby on the A174.

James Cook was born on the 27th of October 1728 in a simple thatched cottage in the village of Marton, 3 miles south of Middlesbrough in Cleveland. He went on to become one of the world's most celebrated maritime explorers. Several sites can still be found which stand testimony to his early formative years in Yorkshire before setting sail around the world. At Marton itself is the Captain Cook Museum and close by is a granite vase marking the site of the family's cottage. On the village green is a stone memorial from Point Hicks in Australia, the first Australian land sighted by Cook.

James, together with his Scottish farmer father and Yorkshire mother, next moved to Airyholme Farm (93: NZ 579/116) in Great Ayton. Their cottage has been moved stone by stone to Melbourne, but a memorial marks the site and the school is now a museum. His mother and five of her other children are buried in All Saints Church.

After working on the farm for a few years he left home in 1744 at the age of 17 to work in a grocer's seafront shop in the old-world fishing village of Staithes. The shop has long since been swept into the sea, but parts of it were re-built into what is now 'Cook's Cottage'. Such are the storms here that a ship's bowsprit is once said to have crashed through the window of the Cod and Lobster Inn!

After 18 months his growing interest in the sea took him to Whitby to be apprenticed to shipowner John Walker, whose vessels took coal to London. Cook lived in Walker's House in Grape Lane, now a museum, and the Whitby Museum in Pannett Park has a Cook Gallery (see no. 35). A statue to Cook stands on the West Cliff overlooking the shipyards where Cook's own ships would later be built. Indeed he never lost touch with Walker or Whitby.

Despite being offered command of a collier, Cook left nine years later to sign up with the Royal Navy. His education and navigational skills saw him progress rapidly through the ranks, especially after he helped chart the St. Lawrence River, enabling Wolfe to secure the capture of Quebec in 1759.

The pinnacle of his career were the famous voyages of exploration. In

The fishing village of Staithes where Captain Cook lived.

1768 in the *Endeavour* he charted New Zealand and Australia's East Coast and in 1772 he took the *Resolution* to the South Pacific in search of a fabled Southern Continent. In 1776, despite considering retirement, he attempted to find a new route to the East Indies, but whilst resting in Hawaii in 1779 was killed trying to resolve an argument between his men and some natives. In 1827 a 50 feet high memorial (93: NZ 590/102) was erected to his memory high on Easby Moor overlooking Great Ayton.

Places of Interest in the Neighbourhood
31. The Planting of the Penny Hedge
34. The Home of England's First Poet
35. A Museumful of Curiosities!
37. The Beggars Bridge

The Beggars Bridge over the Esk in Glaisdale.

37 The Beggars Bridge

Position: Glaisdale (N Yorks)
O.S. Map: Whitby & surrounding area: Sheet No. 94
Map Ref: NZ 783/055
Access: Glaisdale is in the wooded Esk Valley 8 ½ miles south-west of
Whitby off the A171 and the bridge stands a mile to the east between
the railway bridge and the bridge carrying the road to Egton Bridge.

Legend has it that the so-called 'Beggars Bridge' at Glaisdale was truly
a labour of love. During the reign of Elizabeth I a poor young man
of Egton named Thomas Ferris fell in love with a rich girl called
Agnes who lived across the then unbridged River Esk. Tom eventually
declared he would become wealthy enough to build a bridge over the
river, at the same time pleasing Agnes's father who thought him
unsuitable. He became a sailor and ship-owner, fighting the Armada
and visiting America, and eventually became Lord Mayor of Hull. He
also built the bridge, inscribing it with his initials and the date 1619 –
and then he married Agnes!

   In reality the bridge is a typical, humpbacked bridge designed to carry
the long-distance packhorse traffic which criss-crossed the moors and
dales in medieval times. They were economically built with narrow
walkways, and their parapet walls were low and leaning outwards so as
not to hinder the bulky panniers being carried. Also in Eskdale is Duck
Bridge (94: NZ 719/077), downstream from Danby Lodge, which is a
packhorse bridge built in 1386 and repaired in the eighteenth-century
by George Duck. A graceful example crosses the Swale at Ivelet (98: SD
933/978) whose traffic also included bodies on 'the Corpse Way' to the
parish church at Grinton. A large stone on the bank allowed the baskets
to be rested here before crossing.

Places of Interest in the Neighbourhood
28. Always a Warm Welcome!
29. Of Romans and Giants
30. The Railway across the Moors
31. The Planting of the Penny Hedge
35. A Museumful of Curiosities!

38 Tolls and Turnpikes

Position: Osmotherley (N Yorks)
O.S. Map: Northallerton, Ripon & surrounding area: Sheet No. 99
Map Ref: SE 445/994
Access: The Cleveland Tontine Inn is on the junction of the A19 with
the A172 Stokesley road, 1 ½ miles north-west of Osmotherley.

The Turnpike Trust was instigated in England in 1663 in order to
maintain the rapidly deteriorating network of tracks criss-crossing
the country. By exacting a toll from travellers such tracks could be
improved so as to handle the ever-increasing flow of traffic. Tollhouses
were constructed to house the toll-keepers who manned the gate (or
'pike') across the road.

At Aldwark (100: SE 467/622) 11 miles north-west of York, a simple
tollhouse with red, pantiled roof stands just before a bridge over the
River Ure. It is still in operation and a toll-board listing charges can be
seen.

A larger and more ornate tollhouse stands at one end of the Marine
Drive in Scarborough (101: TA 048/893) on the Yorkshire coast. The
road was built to enable people to promenade and take the sea air even
when the tide was in. The tollhouse, built in 1906, resembles a small
castle complete with arch and turret.

Another tollhouse can be seen on Shode Bank at Skipton on the old
Skipton-Ilkley road, 20 miles west of Harrogate on the A59.

A curiosity relating to the turnpike is the Cleveland Tontine Inn near
Osmotherley. The building takes the 'Tontine' of its name from a native
of Naples called Lorenzo Tonti, who in 1653 invented a scheme of life
annuity which increases for the survivors as the subscribers die. In 1804
the Thirsk-Yarm Turnpike was built and the sum of £2,500 was required to erect an inn to serve the stagecoaches using the turnpike. A
number of shares were therefore issued and anyone could buy them
on their own or anyone else's life. The purchaser was thus entitled
to a proportionate share of the profits in their lifetime. When only 3
shareholders remained, the inn was to be theirs in proportion to the
number of shares they held. The inn is a suitably large building with an
elaborate mock-Gothic stable block.

Places of Interest in the Neighbourhood
39. It's a Monk's Life!
40. Where Bulls were once Tethered

39 It's a Monk's Life!

Position: Osmotherley (N Yorks)
O.S. Map: Northallerton, Ripon & surrounding area: Sheet No. 99
Map Ref: SE 449/985
Access: Osmotherley is 5 ½ miles north-east of Northallerton on the
A684 and Mount Grace Priory is a mile to the north. It is an English
Heritage property open all year.

Mount Grace Priory is more properly named 'The House of the
Assumption of the Blessed Virgin Mary and St Nicholas of Mount
Grace in Ingleby'! The fourteenth-century priory is the most important
Carthusian ruin in England and the only one in Yorkshire. Remains of
the cloister, monastic church and the outer court, as well as of some
monastic cells, the gatehouse and tower still survive.

The Carthusian order was particularly strict. The monks only met in
chapel and at religious festivals, otherwise they lived in individual cells,
21 in all, each a tiny 2-storey house with its own garden and workshop.
The cells were 22 feet square and each garden was separated by a high
wall. Meals were received through a hatch in the wall.

Places of Interest in the Neighbourhood
38. Tolls and Turnpikes
40. Where Bulls were once Tethered

A monastic cell and food hatch at Mount Grace Priory.

40 Where Bulls were once Tethered

Position: Northallerton (N Yorks)
O.S. Map: Northallerton, Ripon & surrounding area: Sheet No. 99
Map Ref: SE 367/943
Access: Northallerton is 8 miles north-west of Thirsk on the A168 and
the bull ring is in the market place in the centre of town.

In more barbarous times, the baiting of bulls and bears was a popular
spectator sport. Such events required specially designated areas known
as bull rings, usually in the village square or market place. The term
also referred to a metal ring attached to a large stone sunk deep into the
ground to which the bull to be baited was tethered. The practice was
supposed to tenderise the flesh before slaughter but, thankfully, it was
made illegal in 1835.

However, to remind the visitor of such times the former site of a bull
ring is preserved in the Market Place at Northallerton. Bull rings also
survive in the Market Place at Easingwold (100: SE 528/698) 13 miles
north-west of York, as well as in the village square at Askrigg (98: SD
948/910), 12 miles west of Leyburn, a place once famous for its hand-
knitters.

Cock-fighting took place in hollows in the ground or in depressions
carved out of raised mounds, and an example of the latter survives at
Embsay (104: SE 007/535) 2 miles north-east of Skipton.

Places of Interest in the Neighbourhood
38. Tolls and Turnpikes
39. It's a Monk's Life!

41 An Abbey at the Bottom of the Garden

Position: Rievaulx (N Yorks)
O.S. Map: Malton, Pickering & surrounding area: Sheet No. 100
Map Ref: SE 577/849
Access: Rievaulx Abbey is 2 ½ miles north-west of Helmsley off the B1257 and is an English Heritage property open all year round. Rievaulx Terrace is a National Trust property open from Easter to the end of October.

Rievaulx Abbey was founded in about 1132 in a magnificent rural setting by Cistercian monks from Clairvaux in France. The monastery grew rapidly and the population increased to 140 monks and 500 lay

The beautifully situated ruins of Rievaulx Abbey.

brothers with large farming and industrial estates. However, huge and costly building plans led to debts piling up and the population had fallen to a mere 22 monks by the Dissolution. After the destruction of the Abbey, lead from the roof was buried, not be found until some 400 years later when some was used for repairs of York Minster's 'Five Sisters' window!

The famous Rievaulx Terrace (SE 579/848) nearby is actually an integral part of the landscaping of the Duncombe Park Estate, 2 miles south-east. It was designed by the grandson of Thomas Duncombe in about 1758 and consists of a beautiful ½-mile long grass walk with a Doric temple at one end and an Ionic one at the other. The latter is furnished as a dining room and was used for picnics.

Duncombe Park (SE 604/830) was built in 1713 by the Duncombe family, who moved here from nearby Helmsley Castle. The situation is curiously similar to that at Studley Royal (see no. 69) in that both houses have genuine Abbey ruins in their gardens. After being a school for 60 years it has now reverted to being the home of the Fevershams and is open to the public at certain times of the year.

Duncombe Park also has a terrace with a temple at either end. The northern one is Ionic (c.1730) and thought to be attributed to Vanbrugh, of Castle Howard fame (see no.22). Perhaps there was a plan at some time to join the two terraces together via a bridge over the River Rye because large stones have been found in the river bed. If so the finished walk could have been some 3 miles long – not bad for a stroll down the garden!

Places of Interest in the Neighbourhood
42. Amazing Mazes
43. A Very Odd Book Indeed
44. The Moving History of an Abbey!
45. The 'Mouseman' and the White Horse

42 Amazing Mazes

Position: Dalby (N Yorks)
O.S. Map: Malton, Pickering & surrounding area: Sheet No. 100
Map Ref: SE 626/719
Access: Dalby is 10 miles west of Malton and the maze is on a grass
verge beyond on the way to Brandsby.

All mazes whether lined with hedges or simply cut into turf are
curiosities. The turf maze at Dalby is a rarity because there are now less
than ten turf mazes in Britain and this is Yorkshire's only example.
Called 'The City of Troy', it measures 26 by 22 feet and as such is the
smallest maze in Britain.

   The purpose of these ancient mazes is obscure. They may have been
used in fertility rites, as is suggested by some being called Maiden's
Bowers. Another theory is that they were a means of casting out the
Devil. If the maze was followed from the centre outwards the Devil
could be left behind because he could only travel in straight lines. Local
tradition at Dalby warns of bad luck if one walks the maze more than
nine times.

Places of Interest in the Neighbourhood
22. England's Largest Folly
41. An Abbey at the Bottom of the Garden
43. A Very Odd Book Indeed
44. The Moving History of an Abbey!
45. The 'Mouseman' and the White Horse

A rare turf maze on the roadside at Dalby.

43 A Very Odd Book Indeed

Position: Coxwold (N Yorks)
O.S. Map: Malton, Pickering & surrounding area: Sheet No. 100
Map Ref: SE 532/773
Access: Coxwold is 7½ miles south-east of Thirsk and Shandy Hall is open between June and September on Wednesdays and Sundays.

Shandy Hall at Coxwold was home to the Rev. Laurence Sterne after he received the perpetual curacy there in 1760. The house itself is a fifteenth-century timber-framed hall which was modernised in the seventeenth-century. Its interior is full of curiously-shaped rooms including the small study where he wrote some of *The Life and Opinions of Tristram Shandy, Gentleman.* The house is now a museum and contains the finest collection of first editions of his work.

Sterne was no ordinary country parson. He went to Cambridge University, married a Miss Lumley in 1741, and became vicar in Sutton-in-the-Forest, after a first curacy at Buckden. He wrote the first 2 volumes of *Tristram Shandy,* which despite being attacked for immorality won him the beginnings of a literary reputation. He moved to the curacy at Coxwold, naming his house Shandy Hall, as well as travelling to write *A Sentimental Journey Through France and Italy by Mr Yorick.* Sadly he parted from his wife and daughter, who were supported with the proceeds from his *Sermons.* The concluding volume of *Tristram Shandy* appeared in 1767 and Sterne died in London a year later.

'Tristram Shandy' added a new dimension to the English novel with its innovative style and gentle humour, although some of the satire upset his Yorkshire contemporaries, some of whom thought they recognised themselves in the characters. The book was odd in containing a completely blank page, a black page and a marbled page, and the hero Tristram Shandy is not even born until the end of the book, the 'Life' being that of Sterne's uncle and the 'opinions' those of his father.

Places of Interest in the Neighbourhood
41. An Abbey at the Bottom of the Garden
42. Amazing Mazes
44. The Moving History of an Abbey!
45. The 'Mouseman' and the White Horse
76. Maiden's Garlands

44 The Moving History of an Abbey!

Position: Byland Abbey (N Yorks)
O.S. Map: Malton, Pickering & surrounding area: Sheet No. 100
Map Ref: SE 549/789
Access: Byland Abbey is 8 miles south-east of Thirsk off the A170 near
the village of Coxwold. It is an English Heritage property open all year
round.

The celebrated Byland Abbey has a curious, not to say moving, history.
What we see today are the beautiful picturesque ruins of a twelfth-
century Cistercian Abbey, at one time the largest of its Order in Great
Britain. It was founded by monks from Furness Abbey. They were not
originally Cistercians, but belonged to the Order of Savigny who were
absorbed into the Cistercians in 1147. Byland however was not their
first choice of site. Amongst several early attempts to settle they tried
Ryedale but this proved to be too near to Rievaulx Abbey. The combined effects of the two buildings' sets of bells proved confusing and the
newcomers moved on after only 4 years!

Byland had originally been a village, but the monks relocated this and
rehoused the inhabitants in order to build their church. This was

The well-preserved tiled floors of Byland Abbey.

unusually generous treatment since in some cases the locals were not so fairly treated. The new abbey became part of a large complex with its own road and agricultural and industrial enterprises. The remains, which date from 1170-1225, consist of the magnificent church, lay quarters, kitchen, cellar, warming-house and unusually, no less than five chapels, as well as huge cloisters. There is an interesting museum containing fragments of stonework, proving that the interior was painted white with red outlines. An oddity which has also survived is a gaming board.

Two exterior features which underline the former magnificence of the building are the remains of the huge rose window (at 26 feet across it is one of the largest) and the superb green and yellow glazed floor tiles of what was the earliest, large scale tiled pavement in the country. The magnificent tiled roundel in the chancel should not be missed.

Although Byland was the scene of a battle at which the Scots defeated the English, the Abbey continued to prosper peacefully until the Dissolution of the Monasteries in 1538, when it became derelict.

Places of Interest in the Neighbourhood
41. An Abbey at the Bottom of the Garden
42. Amazing Mazes
43. A Very Odd Book Indeed
45. The 'Mouseman' and the White Horse
76. Maiden's Garlands

The White Horse on the hills above Kilburn.

45 The 'Mouseman' and the White Horse

Position: Kilburn (N Yorks)
O.S. Map: Malton, Pickering & surrounding area: Sheet No. 100
Map Ref: SE 515/813
Access: The village of Kilburn is 7 miles south-east of Thirsk off the A170, and the White Horse is on Roulston Scar in the Hambleton Hills.

Today Kilburn is world famous as the home of carpenter Robert Thompson. His nick-name, 'The Mouseman', alludes to his trademark of a tiny carved mouse which appears on much of his fine oak wood-work. Examples of his work can be found in, amongst many other places, Ampleforth Abbey, All Saints church at Brandsby and the Regimental Chapel of the Green Howards in St Mary's at Richmond. His work is continued to this day by his successors, and the medieval chapel of St Thomas in St Mary's Church at Kilburn was re-furbished in 1958 as a memorial to him.

In the hillside above Kilburn can be found the huge figure of a white horse, put there in 1857 by locally born Thomas Taylor who ran a successful London grocery business. His shop was noted for York hams and other delicacies and it was while out searching for these that he was greatly impressed by the ancient Uffington White Horse in Berkshire. Taylor may even have attended the seven-yearly 'scouring' (cleaning) which took place in 1857. Immediately he set about planning a similar horse for his home village. 30 men were involved, led by the local school master, and some 6 tons of lime were needed for the whitewashing since the hill is not composed of chalk. The figure is 314 feet long and 228 feet high, and no less than 20 people can sit on the horse's eye alone! It is said that a hailstorm in 1896 nearly erased it.

Places of Interest in the Neighbourhood
41. An Abbey at the Bottom of the Garden
42. Amazing Mazes
43. A Very Odd Book Indeed
44. The Moving History of an Abbey!

46 A Superlative Market Town

Position: Richmond (N Yorks)
O.S. Map: Barnard Castle & surrounding area: Sheet No. 92
Map Ref: NZ 172/011
Access: Richmond is 4½ miles south-west of Scotch Corner on the
A6108. The Castle is an English Heritage property open all year round.

Richmond is a fine town which can boast one of the largest market
places in the county. It is dominated by the impressive Norman castle
(NZ 174/006), a triangular structure begun in c.1071 by Alan 'The
Red'. The keep, one of the finest in the country, was added on top of the
original gatehouse by Henry II a hundred years later. It is a hundred
feet high with walls 11 feet thick. However, the fact that the castle has
survived in such good condition to this day owes much to its never
being tested by siege.

Places of Interest in the Neighbourhood
60. A Churchful of Curiosities
61. The Bridge Brought Down by a Herd of Cows!

The mighty keep of Richmond Castle.

47 Monument to a Massacre

Position: Richmond (N Yorks)
O.S. Map: Barnard Castle & surrounding area: Sheet No. 92
Map Ref: NZ 167/006
Access: Richmond is 4½ miles south-west of Scotch Corner on the
A6108. The Culloden Tower is in a park by the side of the River Swale
just outside the town but is only open occasionally (see the Tourist
Office for details).

The Yorke family were an old established Richmond family who repre-
sented the Borough in Parliament. Although their mansion has long
since been demolished their grounds still provide pretty walks running
down to the River Swale. Here can be found the Temple Lodge, a
Gothic style, castellated mansion built for John Yorke in 1769. More
interesting is the Culloden Tower (or Cumberland Temple) on a knoll
between the lodge and the river. This folly was erected in 1747, a year
after the battle of the same name, in which Joseph Yorke, son of
John, had fought. The English vanquished the Scottish Jacobite rebels
although their victory was forever marred by the Duke of Cumberland's order to massacre all those linked with the rebellion. The tower is

The Culloden Tower at Richmond.

an 8-sided Gothic structure set on a square base with an attached turret containing a staircase. Although many follies are plain inside, the Culloden Tower is finely decorated and well preserved, having been renovated by The Landmark Trust as one of their unusual holiday properties. Ironically it was built on the site of a tower used to safeguard cattle during the Scottish incursions in the time of Edward II.

Less elaborate but more curious is the oddly named 'Oliver Duckett' folly (NZ 183/022) on the roadside a mile north-east of Richmond on the B6274. It was once thought that Duckett was a local name for a dovecote, though it is more likely to have been a house lived in by an Oliver Duckett. If so, it is one of those rare follies to be named after a person.

Places of Interest in the Neighbourhood
46. A Superlative Market Town
48. Lost Lead Mines of the Dales
60. A Churchful of Curiosities
61. The Bridge Brought Down by a Herd of Cows!

The powder house at Langthwaite in Arkengarthdale.

48 Lost Lead Mines of the Dales

Position: Langthwaite (N Yorks)
O.S. Map: Barnard Castle & surrounding area: Sheet No. 92
Map Ref: NZ 998/035
Access: Langthwaite is in Arkengarthdale which runs north of Reeth in Swaledale. The powder magazine stands alone in a field beyond the 'C.B.' inn, on the right.

The idyllic and peaceful landscape of the Yorkshire Dales which we see today was once witness to considerable industrial exploitation, most notably lead mining.

After the heavy ore had been mined it was refined on-site in order to reduce it to a manageable weight before being transported away. This was done in smelting mills whose ghostly remains can be seen today. They contained great arched furnaces heated with the use of water-powered bellows.

Swaledale was one such lead mining centre where, near the village of Marrick (99: SE 075/984) can be seen the Upper Smelting Mill (c.1860) with great arches over the furnace hearths and a chimney rising above. Another smelt mill (c.1820) at Grinton (98: SE 050/964) near Reeth has nearby it a flue which runs up the hillside to carry the fumes away from the mill. Also here is a peat store where fuel for the furnaces was kept dry. Further examples are the Surrender Smelt Mill (92: NY 988/003) in nearby Arkengarthdale and the smelt mill at Blakethwaite Mine (92: NY 937/018) in Gunnerside. On the hillsides can sometimes be seen great exposed areas ("hushes") where deliberately impounded water was allowed to flood down removing the topsoil ready for mining.

To facilitate blasting, black powder was used which because of its volatile nature had to be kept in an isolated building. The greatest curiosity associated with lead mining is the quaint, hexagonal powder house in Arkengarthdale (see above for access) which looks more like a tiny chapel. Built in 1804 it was part of the 'C.B.' mines named after their founder Charles Bathurst.

Places of Interest in the Neighbourhood
49. A Blast at Bedtime
58. The Rocket Ship and other Odd Buildings
59. An Ancient Yorkshire Game
60. A Churchful of Curiosities

49 A Blast at Bedtime

Position: Bainbridge (N Yorks)
O.S. Map: Wensleydale & Upper Wharfedale: Sheet No. 98
Map Ref: SD 934/904
Access: Bainbridge is situated in Wensleydale on the A684 4 miles east of Hawes and the Rose and Crown public house is on the village green.

One of the longest-lived English customs is that of horn-blowing. At Bainbridge on winter evenings between the end of September and Shrove Tuesday, a horn is blown at 9 p.m. This is a tradition passed down by members of the Metcalfe family who live in the family's fortified farmhouse, Nappa Hall (SE 966/905). A buffalo horn is used today but there is also a cow horn. They are kept in the Rose and Crown, an ancient local inn dating from 1445. The horn is also blown at weddings for good luck.

The purpose of this evening sounding is lost in antiquity but may have been to summon the sheep and guide the shepherd in the dark. It may also have guided travellers to shelter through the once wild forest.

A horn-blowing ceremony known as 'Setting the Watch' occurs at Ripon 26 miles to the south-east on the A61. Ripon's charter was granted in 886 by King Alfred in the form of a horn, a copy of which is blown by the chief officer (or Wakeman) every night at 9 p.m. in the market place and outside the house of the Mayor. The Wakeman then kept watch until dawn and anyone robbed during this time was eligible for compensation. At the same time as the horn is blown a curfew bell in the cathedral is rung.

Talking of bells, daily at Richmond 20 miles north up the A1, at 8 a.m. and 8 p.m., a curfew bell is rung signalling the start and finish of the apprentices' workday, and hence is called the 'prentices' bell'. The bell in Trinity Church is now automatic, but originally the town crier's house was at the foot of the tower.

Places of Interest in the Neighbourhood

50 Survivals of the Reformation

Position: Hubberholme (N Yorks)
O.S. Map: Wensleydale & Upper Wharfedale: Sheet No. 98
Map Ref: SE 926/783
Access: The village of Hubberholme is in Langstrothdale, in Upper Wharfedale, 8 miles south-east of Hawes just off the B6160.

Hubberholme is named after a Viking chieftain and has a very old church with a squat thirteenth-century tower. The greatest treasure in the church of St. Michael is a rare 'rood loft' dating from 1558, one of only two such examples in Yorkshire. The loft takes the form of an elaborately carved, wooden balcony supported by pillars whose purpose was to support the 'rood', or crucifix. During the Reformation most were ripped out as part of the campaign to eradicate Roman Catholic 'popery'. The arms of the Percy family and the date can be seen carved onto the loft. The church also contains pews and choir

The rare 'Roof Loft' in the church at Hubberholme.

stalls carved by the 'Mouseman' Robert Thompson of Kilburn (see no. 45), a stained glass window depicting episodes of local history and a memorial to Bradford born author J.B. Priestley (1894-1984), who was particularly fond of Hubberholme.

Over the nearby bridge is the George Inn, once the vicarage, where on New Year's Day the Hubberholme 'Parliament' met. Local farmers bid for the tenancy of Kirkgill pasture and the proceeds went to the parish needy. The bar was dubbed the House of Commons and another room, occupied by the Church Wardens, was called the House of Lords, where it was decided how the money should be spent.

Yorkshire's other rood loft is in St Oswald's Church at Flamborough in Humberside (101: TA 226/702) 3 miles north-east of Bridlington. It is thought to be fifteenth-century and comprises a series of carved and canopied niches. Also in the church is a fine and long inscription in English verse to Sir Marmaduke Constable referring to the battle of Brankiston (Flodden Field) in 1513.

Places of Interest in the Neighbourhood
49. A Blast at Bedtime
56. Scenery that Inspired *The Water Babies*
57. A Haunt of Early Farming Folk
58. The Rocket Ship and other Odd Buildings

The ruined Hoffman Kiln at Langcliffe.

51 The Kiln as Big as a Castle

Position: Langcliffe (N Yorks)
O.S. Map: Wensleydale and Upper Wharfedale: Sheet No. 98
Map Ref: SD 812/653
Access: Langcliffe village is in Ribblesdale 1 mile north of Settle on the B6479, and the kiln is beyond next to the railway up a road signposted to a refuse tip.

The village of Langcliffe, meaning long cliff, was mentioned in the Domesday Book and was given to a Cistercian order of monks by Elias of Giggleswick. In 1318 a raid by the Scots proved so violent as to necessitate the rebuilding of the village on a new site.

The true curiosity here, however, relates to industrial archaeology. On the riverside near to the old cotton mill (1851) with its attendant weirs can be found the enormous Hoffman Kiln. These unique remains were once the site of lime-burning on a massive scale. Although the kiln, built from a German design, is now derelict and overrun with weeds, much of its original construction can be seen. It is circular in plan with a circumference of 150 feet, the brick outer walls looking more like a castle than a kiln. Inside were 16 chambers where limestone was burned, the resulting lime being sold for use in furnaces, tanneries and buildings. Eventually new technology and chemicals rendered the kiln obsolete.

Places of Interest in the Neighbourhood
52. Settle Enigmas!
53. England's Earliest Semi!
56. Scenery that Inspired *The Water Babies*

52 Settle Enigmas!

Position: Settle (N Yorks)
O.S. Map: Wensleydale & Upper Wharfedale: Sheet No. 98
Map Ref: SD 818/635
Access: Settle is 14 miles north-west of Skipton on the A65.

A plaque set in the wall of the 'Naked Man Cafe' depicts a man holding
what appears to be a carpenter's plane in front of him and surrounded
by a coffin shape. He is known as the naked man, but is actually
wearing knee-breeches and a buttoned tunic. Curiously enough, on a
wall at Cross Green in Langcliffe (SD 823/650) a mile north of Settle, is
a carving known as the naked lady. Both signs are dated to the
seventeenth-century and are thought to be signs for undertakers or
carpenters.

   Settle has a shambles, as has York, and nearby is a very odd house
known as The Folly (1675-9), most likely because it cost the builder
Thomas Preston so much money that he had to leave it unfinished.
Basically it is in the vernacular style but with the West Riding tradition
of adding decorative and fanciful additions.

Places of Interest in the Neighbourhood
51. The Kiln as Big as a Castle
53. England's Earliest Semi!
56. Scenery that Inspired *The Water Babies*

The 'Naked Man' on a wall in Settle.

53 England's Earliest Semi!

Position: Arnford (N Yorks)
O.S. Map: Blackburn, Burnley & surrounding area: Sheet No. 103
Map Ref: SD 837/563
Access: Arnford is 1 ¼ miles west of Hellifield, 5 miles south-east of Settle and is reached down a track off the A682. The house is private and there is strictly no access.

There is a curious farm house at Arnford which is thought to be the earliest semi-detached house in England. Built between 1690-1700 it was from the start designed as a double house – possibly for 2 brothers? It has eight windows along the facade and two gabled doorways. The gables themselves are unusual in having odd two-light windows with round-headed windows above. Each house still has its original fireplace in a room adjacent to the doorway and each has a staircase in the room behind.

Reputedly England's earliest 'semi' at Arnford.

Other ancient Yorkshire buildings include Richmond Castle, 4½ miles south-west of Scotch Corner, where Scolland's Hall dating to c.1080 is possibly the oldest surviving domestic building in England (see no. 46). Meanwhile at Grassington, 7½ miles north of Skipton, the Hall (98: SE 004/640) behind the square is reputed to be the oldest continually inhabited house in Yorkshire, dating from the late thirteenth-century.

Places of Interest in the Neighbourhood
51. The Kiln as Big as a Castle
52. Settle Enigmas!
54. The Relentless Restorer of Castles
56. Scenery that Inspired *The Water Babies*

The gatehouse of Skipton Castle.

54 The Relentless Restorer of Castles

Position: Skipton (N Yorks)
O.S. Map: Blackburn, Burnley & surrounding area: Sheet No. 103
Map Ref: SD993/519
Access: Skipton is 20 miles west of Harrogate on the A59 and the Castle is at the head of the High Street. It is privately owned but open to the public all year round.

Skipton Castle is eleventh-century, but virtually the only Norman fabric remaining is the arched west doorway leading into the central conduit court where water was collected. It belonged to the Clifford family from medieval times onwards and consisted of an inner bailey with curtain walls and towers, some of which are circular. It is Yorkshire's only castle which bears any similarity to the concentric planned castles of Edward I. Such was its strength that it withstood the Parliamentarians' siege for 3 years during the Civil War before being finally captured and pulled down. It would have remained ruinous had not the redoubtable Lady Anne Clifford rebuild it in 1657, as she did half a dozen other castles as well as a dozen or so churches (see no. 55). So that the castle could never again be defended militarily she was only permitted walls thinner than the originals. During World War II many valuable manuscripts and artworks were stored here for safety. An oddly attractive feature is the shell-lined grotto built in the 1620's inside the fourteenth-century gatehouse. The Guernsey Ormer shells and Jamaican coral are said to have been collected by Anne's father the Elizabethan George Clifford, 3rd Earl of Cumberland, on one of his expeditions as an admiral.

Lady Anne Clifford also restored Holy Trinity Church in Skipton in 1655. Dating from the reign of Richard III it too was damaged in the Civil War. It contains many Clifford monuments including a tomb which acts as the altar. Remains of an anchorite cell can be found near the west end of the north wall.

Places of Interest in the Neighbourhood
53. England's Earliest Semi!
55. Lady Clifford's Circular Almshouse
56. Scenery that Inspired *The Water Babies*
57. A Haunt of Early Farming Folk

55 Lady Clifford's Circular Almshouse

Position: Beamsley (N Yorks)
O.S. Map: Leeds, Bradford & Harrogate area: Sheet No. 104
Map Ref: SE 083/531
Access: Beamsley is 4 miles north-west of Ilkley along the A65 and
B6160, and the almshouses are reached by turning right at Bolton
Bridge along the A59 Harrogate road. They are reached through an
arched entrance on the roadside.

The almshouses at Beamsley are remarkable for the inclusion of an
unusual circular hospital founded in 1593 by Margaret Russell, Countess of Cumberland. The present shape we see today was evidently
created some 60 years later by the redoubtable Lady Anne Clifford,
Countess of Pembroke, who finished it 'more profusely' (see no. 54).
  Fronting the road is a conventional, two-storey range of almshouses
with an arched gate-house displaying the Clifford family coat of arms.
However, a path beyond the arch leads through a garden to the circular
Hospital building, 30 feet in diameter, with a lantern-topped conical
roof (see front cover). Directly below the lantern is a Chapel which still
retains its wooden pews, pulpit and Beamsley Bible. Set around the
chapel are seven rooms for seven almswomen, with four chimney stacks
on the dividing walls.
  Beamsley Hospital is an extraordinary building for its date, and continued to house old people until recently, when they were re-located to
Skipton. The building is now the property of the Landmark Trust, but it
can be viewed from the outside.

Places of Interest in the Neighbourhood
54. The Relentless Restorer of Castles
57. A Haunt of Early Farming Folk
68. One Down, Two to Go!

56 Scenery that Inspired *The Water Babies*

Position: Malham (N Yorks)
O.S. Map: Wensleydale & Upper Wharfedale: Sheet No. 98
Map Ref: SD 89/64
Access: The village of Malham is 5 ½ miles east of Settle in Upper Craven, midway between Ribblesdale to the west and Wharfedale to the east. Malham Cove is 3/4 of a mile north and its surroundings are a National Trust property open all year round.

Malham Cove, Malham Tarn (SD 89/66) 2 miles beyond, and Goredale Scar (SD 91/64) 2 miles north-east of Malham, together form one of the most curious and spectacular natural vistas in the north of England.

The Cove is a huge, semicircular amphitheatre of limestone cliffs some 240 feet high. Prior to the Ice Age the River Aire flowed over the edge of the cove in a huge waterfall which would have been higher than Niagara. Today the river emerges at the base of the cliffs, having seeped through fissures at the top.

Goredale Scar is a picturesque gorge forming part of the same Craven Fault. Goredale Beck leaps the cliffs here in two huge cascades. Malham Tarn is a 150 acre natural lake and is the highest in the Pennines.

An unusual feature of the so-called Great Scar landscape are the limestone pavements patterned by 'clints' or 'grykes' splitting the surface into blocks, the result of millenia of water and ice erosion.

The Cove is unclimbable without artifical aids and inspired Charles Kingsley to write his novel *The Water Babies*. In it his boy chimney-sweep Tom falls over the edge. A local legend tells of a seventeenth-century witch who leapt over the edge only to be saved by her broomstick!

Malham Tarn House was owned by Walter Morrison, a friend of Charles Kingsley as well as of Ruskin and Darwin.

Places of Interest in the Neighbourhood
50. Survivals of the Reformation
51. The Kiln as Big as a Castle
52. Settle Enigmas!
53. England's Earliest Semi!
57. A Haunt of Early Farming Folk

57 A Haunt of Early Farming Folk

Position: Grassington (N Yorks)
O.S.Map: Wensleydale & Upper Wharfedale: Sheet No. 98
Map Ref: SE 003/648
Access: Grassington is in Wharfedale 8 miles north of Skipton on the
A6265. The Iron Age settlement remains are on the limestone plateau
immediately north of the village, reached by bearing left at the top of
the main street and following the second lane on the right.

Grassington is one of the oldest inhabited places in the Dales and the
area abounds with antiquities. There is evidence from the Bronze and
Iron Ages, the Roman period, the Middle Ages and beyond.

From the Bronze Age we have round burial mounds (or 'barrows') but
more important are the extensive Iron Age camps, fields and settle-
ments to the east of the Pateley Bridge road. Circular hut enclosures
have been found containing Iron Age remains and they adjoin typical
Iron Age fields. In establishing fields, these early farmers looked to the
slopes rather than the valley bottom, which was too marshy for cultiva-
tion. Here they collected boulders and laid them out to form small
rectangular plots ('Celtic Fields') ½ – 2 acres in size which were then
ploughed. Repeated ploughing caused the soil to creep down the slopes
and build up against the downslope boundaries, ultimately creating the
characteristic terraced banks (or 'Lynchets') which can be seen today.
Iron Age finds from Grassington can be seen in the Craven Museum at
Skipton.

The name Grassington means 'the pasture farm' in Anglo-Saxon and
it was they who colonised Wharfedale and continued to terrace the
slopes to produce fields. As the common field system broke down so
the gradual enclosure of the Dales into walled fields occurred. This
was to denote ownership and prevent trespass and continued until the
early nineteenth-century, creating the patchwork effect so typical of the
Dales today. The long runs of dry stone walls in the area are often only
broken by self-shutting gates, stepped stiles, 'squeeze-bellies' (narrow
breaks in the wall to allow people to pass), and 'sheep creeps' or 'cripple
holes' (to allow sheep through). The Upper Wharfedale Museum in
Market Square illustrates fully the area's farming history.

Places of Interest in the Neighbourhood
50. Survivals of the Reformation
56. Scenery that Inspired *'The Water Babies'*

58 The Rocket Ship and other Odd Buildings

Position: Aysgarth (N Yorks)
O.S. Map: Wensleydale & Upper Wharfedale: Sheet No. 98
Map Ref: SE 027/883
Access: Aysgarth is in Wensleydale 8 ½ miles west of Middleham on the A684 and Sorrel Sykes Park is reached from the B6160. The park is private but the follies are visible from the road.

Aysgarth is renowned for its famous waterfalls, but of greater curiosity is Sorrel Sykes Park. Sorrel Sykes farm is in fact a mansion built c.1750. It is unusual in having a modest facade fronting the road but that of a grand Palladian mansion facing the park to the rear. The park comprises a steep ridge bounded by a lawn, originally dominated by an eagle-topped column. This was accidently toppled by a tractor in the

The 'Rocket Ship' at Aysgarth.

1980's! Nearby is a sham ruin masking the site of an eighteenth-century lead mine comprising an arch and window with romantically crumbling walls. The ruin is mirrored to the north by the very real Castle Bolton (SE 034/917), built in the fourteenth-century to guard Wensleydale. In a field beyond are three follies said to have been erected by redundant mill workers on the instruction of the then lady of the house. These comprise a cone-shaped smoke hole built in 1921, a tiny arched gateway, and the locally named 'Rocket Ship'. This is a tapered tower on a square, buttressed base containing a single room. On the opposite side of the road is a private farmhouse with a tall and ornate terracotta chimney pot in the front garden. This was transported here in two army trucks from the Home Counties by a retired Major as a souvenir!

Returning east along the A684, just before Swinithwaite, is Temple Farm. Over a high wall on the north side of the road, concealed by trees, is a garden temple built by John Foss in 1792 for nearby Swinithwaite Hall. Octagonal in shape, it rises two storeys and has the sculpture of a dog over the door. The name of the farm refers to a Knights Templar Chapel which once existed nearby.

Places of Interest in the Neighbourhood
49. A Blast at Bedtime
50. Survivals of the Reformation
59. An Ancient Yorkshire Game
60. A Churchful of Curiosities
61. The Bridge Brought Down by a Herd of Cows!

59 An Ancient Yorkshire Game

Position: Redmire (N Yorks)
O.S. Map: Wensleydale & Upper Wharfedale: Sheet No. 98
Map Ref: SE 045/913
Access: Redmire is in Wensleydale 10 miles south-west of Richmond off the A6108 and the quoits pitch is near the old market cross.

The ancient Yorkshire game of quoits was once commonplace during summer evenings on the village greens and in the public house yards of North Yorkshire. A set of quoits would also be kept on most farms for those rare occasions when time and weather permitted their use.

A quoits pitch was typically 11 yards long, although some were as much as 18 yards. At each end was a square bed of clay (the 'box') in which an iron post (or 'hob') was fixed. The game involved two men in a knockout tournament throwing a specially bevelled metal ring (or 'quoit') from post to post. It is said to be a tactical game of great skill and strength. Sometimes old horseshoes were used. To decide who throws first a quoit is tossed in the air and one player calls 'ill' or 'owl' (hill or hole). This was in reference to the bevelled or non-bevelled faces of the quoit. The first competitor then throws, scoring a point if he gets his quoit nearest the hob. Two points (a 'ringer') is scored should the quoit land right over the hob.

Quoits can still be seen today at country shows and in some villages such as Redmire, on the edge of the Yorkshire Dales National Park. On the green at nearby Castle Bolton (SE 034/918) the tradition of 'poddling in' was used to decide teams. A walking stick was laid on the floor and the contestants threw a handy object, such as a penknife or pencil, as near as possible to it. The pairs of objects landing closest together decided who played with whom. At feast time some three dozen games were played lasting three or four days with copper kettles as prizes.

Places of Interest in the Neighbourhood
48. Lost Lead Mines of the Dales
49. A Blast at Bedtime
58. The Rocket Ship and other Odd Buildings
60. A Churchful of Curiosities
61. The Bridge Brought down by a Herd of Cows!

60 A Churchful of Curiosities

Position: Wensley (N Yorks)
O.S. Map: Northallerton, Ripon & surrounding area: Sheet No. 99
Map Ref: SE 092/895
Access: Wensley is situated in Wensleydale 1 ½ miles south-west of
Leyburn on the A684.

Holy Trinity Church in Wensley is a fascinating place in that it
represents 700 years both of spasmodic building and of accumulating
curious fittings. The oldest part of the church is the chancel which is
mid-thirteenth-century and contains a fine carved stone 'sedilia' (clergy
seat) and 'piscina' (basin for washing communion vessels).

The church is crammed with interesting features, the oldest of which
are two pieces of a ninth-century Anglo-Saxon cross. On the north-wall
can be found traces of early fourteenth-century wall painting depicting
the Three Quick and the Three Dead. There is also a fine Flemish brass
to a priest, Sir Simon de Wenslaw, dated 1394.

Near the north door is a large wooden box said to be a fifteenth-
century 'reliquary' from Easby Abbey to which is attached a lockable
'poor box'. It is said to have held the bones of St Agatha. Similarly
acquired is the early sixteenth-century screenwork re-used as part of the
seventeenth-century Scrope family pew, complete with its own curtains
for privacy.

Places of Interest in the Neighbourhood
58. The Rocket Ship and other Odd Buildings
59. An Ancient Yorkshire Game
61. The Bridge Brought Down By a Herd of Cows!

*The ancient 'reliquary' box in
Wensley Church.*

61 The Bridge Brought Down by a Herd of Cows!

Position: Middleham (N Yorks)
O.S. Map: Northallerton, Ripon & surrounding area: Sheet No. 99
Map Ref: SE 119/888
Access: Middleham is 17 miles north-west of Ripon on the A6108 and the bridge crosses the River Ure a mile further to the north-west.

One of the country's earliest suspension bridges was built at Middleham in 1829 by Joseph Aloysius Hanson, the inventor of the Hanson Cab, and Edward Welch. Unfortunately the design was faulty and it reputedly collapsed when a herd of cows crossing it fell into step causing disastrous vibrations. It was later converted to a cast iron girder bridge which looks out of keeping with the idiosyncratic towers which once held the suspension cables. The towers were medievalised by the addition of mock castellations and arrowslits.

Places of Interest in the Neighbourhood
58. The Rocket Ship and Other Odd Buildings
60. A Churchful of Curiosities
62. Where Abbots Preserved their Dignity!
63. Bee Boles and 'Old Peculier'
64. Yorkshire's Stonehenge

The former suspension bridge outside Middleham.

62 Where Abbots Preserved their Dignity!

Position: Jervaulx (N Yorks)
O.S. Map: Northallerton, Ripon & surrounding area: Sheet No. 99
Map Ref: SE 173/858
Access: Jervaulx Abbey is signposted off the A6108 between Masham and East Witton and is a Department of the Environment property open to the public.

At the entrance to Jervaulx Abbey is a very curious survival in the form of a stone embalming slab. It was apparently used when the corpses of abbots and other notables of the Abbey were being embalmed. It is still possible to see the positioning space where the head was placed and a drain at the other end for the bodily fluids.

The Abbey itself is one of that superb series of Cistercian abbeys whose remains still grace the North Yorkshire landscape. It was founded in 1156 AD and its first Abbot was John de Kinston who, it is said, while travelling from Byland Abbey, had a vision of Christ and the Virgin Mary who bade him found an abbey at Yorevak.

Jervaulx, as it was subsequently called, became a power in the area, owning much of Wensleydale. The monks became excellent horse-breeders - the Middleham area is today still famous for this – and wealthy from wool and cheese manufacture. They made the famous Wensleydale cheese from ewes' milk, and a cheese press can still be seen at Askrigg.

The work of the Abbey was ended abruptly during the Dissolution of the Monasteries under Henry VIII. The buildings fell into disrepair and much of the fine stonework was removed for local houses, so that the remains are largely domestic although the site of the church remains.

Places of Interest in the Neighbourhood
60. A Churchful of Curiosities
61. The Bridge Brought Down by a Herd of Cows!
63. Bee Boles and 'Old Peculier'
64. Yorkshire's Stonehenge
65. A Romantic Folly Garden

63 Bee Boles and 'Old Peculier'

Position: Masham (N Yorks)
O.S. Map: Northallerton, Ripon & surrounding area: Sheet No. 99
Map Ref: SE 230/788
Access: Masham is 8 miles north-west of Ripon on the A6108 from
where Nutwith Cote is reached via a road running south.

Nutwith Cote Farm is a small, four-bayed mansion known also as Old
Swinton Hall. Its chief curiosity is an outbuilding the base of which
contains a row of 'beeboles'. These are recesses in which bee-keepers
placed their straw hives (or skeps) for warmth and protection against
the elements. The word beebole is derived from a Scots word for a wall
recess and is also known in Yorkshire as a bee-house. Such sturdily and
carefully constructed beeboles as these are decidely rare. However, a
more modest example exists in a garden wall at West Scrafton in Cover-
dale, and there is an example of a bee alcove, in which three hives are
placed one above the other on shelves, in a garden at Sedbusk near
Hawes. A set of eight bee alcoves is built into a hillside in a field at
Hurst, west of Richmond. Curiously enough the earliest example of a

Beeboles at Nutwith Cote Farm near Masham.

straw skep was found at the Coppergate excavations in York and dates from the twelfth-century.

Nutwith Cote was once a resting place for monks travelling between the abbeys of Jervaulx and Fountains and local legend tells of a secret tunnel they built under the River Ure. Beyond the farm is a now ruined classical dovecote set on a hillock.

Nearby Masham has achieved international fame as the home of Theakstons Old Peculier beer, named after the Peculier of Masham, a medieval official. It is brewed in a small family brewery (SE 224/816) founded in 1827 and comprising a stone-built complex with fine maltings.

Places of Interest in the Neighbourhood
62. Where Abbots Preserved Their Dignity
64. Yorkshire's Stonehenge
65. A Romantic Folly Garden
66. A Truly Illuminating Story
67. A Landowner's Lookout Tower

A mock Stonehenge in the woods at Ilton.

64 Yorkshire's Stonehenge

Position: Ilton (N Yorks)
O.S. Map: Northallerton, Ripon & surrounding area: Sheet No. 99
Map Ref: SE 175/787
Access: The village of Ilton is 3 miles south-west of Masham on the A6108. The stone circle is set in a clearing on Forestry Commision land called Druids Wood reached from a minor road a mile north-west of Ilton.

The so-called Druids circle at Ilton is the finest example of a number of sham Stonehenges in Britain (see back cover). It was built to the orders of William Danby (1752-1833) of Swinton Hall to give work to the unemployed, who were paid a shilling a day. Danby was also a good landlord, allowing visitors to view his estate, but he was also the eccentric author of four volumes of 'Thoughts'.

An avenue of standing stones leads to the circle, which is dominated by a fanciful monolith on a three-tiered base. The structure owes its design to the interest in Druids fashionable in the early nineteenth-century.

An old local story runs that the builder of the circle would provide food and an annuity to anyone who could live in silence at the circle for 7 years, letting their hair and beard grow freely. It is said that one contender lasted 4½ years before giving up.

A true stone circle, though not now as visually striking, is Standing-stones Rigg (101: SE 983/969) 6 miles north-west of Scarborough off the A171. It is 32 feet in diameter and originally had 24 standing stones. A burial chamber was in the centre, stones from which are in the museum at Scarborough.

Places of Interest in the Neighbourhood
62. Where Abbots Preserved their Dignity
63. Bee Boles and 'Old Peculier'
65. A Romantic Folly Garden
66. A Truly Illuminating Story
67. A Landowner's Lookout Tower

65 A Romantic Folly Garden

Position: Grewelthorpe (N Yorks)
O.S.Map: Northallerton, Ripon & surrounding area: Sheet No. 99
Map Ref: SE 233/775
Access: Grewelthorpe is 3 miles south of Masham and the folly garden is in Hackfall Woods in the Ure gorge to the north-east. It is accessible from the village of Mickley.

John Aislabie was head of a revered and gentrified local family, and was Chancellor of the Exchequer in the early eighteenth-century. Together with his son William and head gardener William Fisher he used much of his great wealth to build the beautiful, follified estate at Studley Royal (see no. 69). However, by 1750 William, as well as maintaining his father's estate, had his sights set on executing his own grand designs. To this end he began work in the steep, isolated Ure gorge near Grewelthorpe which his family owned. Hackfall Woods (or Hag's Vale, haunt of witches) thus became England's first 'Romantic' garden, complete with twisting river, crags and wooded glens. Right up until early this century coaches from Harrogate brought tourists to it.

At the entrance is Kents Seat, a stone-built resting place facing the once gushing Alumn Cascade. Beyond is a shell-lined grotto named Fisher's Hall after the gardener, who died in 1743. Octagonal in shape, it has a stone over the doorway inscribed 'W.A. 1750'.

Further to the north is the garden's centrepiece called the Fountain Plain, although the pond is now stagnant and the fountains silent. On the banks are a grotto, a boulder-built rustic temple and a broken obelisk erected by the Victorian owner Lord Ripon.

Above the Fountain Plain on the north boundary of the estate is a Graeco-Roman folly called Mowbray Point Banqueting House. One side faces the fields, while the other fakes a vaulted Roman ruin. Meanwhile up on the cliffs forming the southern boundary of the estate is Mowbray Castle. This sham ruin was built as an eyecatcher to be seen from a distance and was named after the De Mowbrays, a local family of warring medieval knights.

Although today the gardens are in decay, the trees felled and the buildings crumbling, it remains a fascinating, if haunted, place.

Places of Interest in the Neighbourhood
63. Bee Boles and 'Old Peculier'
64. Yorkshire's Stonehenge

66 A Truly Illuminating Story!

Position: West Tanfield (N Yorks)
O.S. Map: Northallerton, Ripon & surrounding area: Sheet No. 99
Map Ref: SE 269/788
Access: West Tanfield is 5 ½ miles north-west of Ripon on the A6108 and Tanfield Hall is on the riverside next to the church and the Marmion Tower.

In 1871 Miss Elizabeth Clarke of Tanfield Hall married the splendidly named Colonel Rookes Everly Bell Crompton. The Colonel was an ingenious and practical fellow who was to play a key role in the development of electric lighting. He began modestly by illuminating the Hall of his new in-laws by means of a generator powered by a waterwheel on the nearby River Ure. When he moved to London his house there was the first to be entirely lit by electricity, a task he was soon employed to do at Buckingham Palace and Windsor Castle. He finally gained fame and fortune by lighting up the city of Vienna.

Other curiosities at West Tanfield include a lofty fifteenth-century gatehouse which is all that remains of a castle owned by the Marmion family who were made famous in a Sir Walter Scott novel. Not only curious but unique is the fourteenth-century alabaster Marmion tomb in St Nicholas's Church. This has a wrought iron canopy (or 'hearse') to support the pall and along the top are spikes to hold candles – a rare survival. In the church porch are a set of dog tethers to which animals were tied while their owners prayed.

Places of Interest in the Neighbourhood
63. Bee Boles and 'Old Peculier'
64. Yorkshire's Stonehenge
65. A Romantic Folly Garden
67. A Landowner's Lookout Tower
71. An Anglo-Saxon Treasure House

67 A Landowner's Lookout Tower

Position: Azerley (N Yorks)
O.S. Map: Northallerton, Ripon & surrounding area: Sheet No. 99
Map Ref: SE 266/743
Access: The hamlet of Azerley is 4 miles north-west of Ripon between Sutton Grange and Grewelthorpe and the tower is reached from a minor road running south.

The tower at Azerley is visible on the skyline from all around being surrounded, as it is, by empty fields. It is square in shape with three small windows set one above the other and rising to a castellated top. Once closer, it can be seen to rise from the roof of a small Victorian bungalow, like an outsize chimney. Little is known of the tower's origins but a story runs that a local landowner once used it as an observation tower from which to survey his labourers at work!

Places of Interest in the Neighbourhood
63. Bee Boles and 'Old Peculier'
65. A Romantic Folly Garden
66. A Truly Illuminating Story
69. Britain's most Beautiful Abbey
71. An Anglo-Saxon Treasure House

A landowner's observation tower at Azerley.

68 One Down, Two to Go!

Position: Pateley Bridge (N Yorks)
O.S. Map: Northallerton, Ripon & surrounding area: Sheet No. 99
Map Ref: SE 158/635
Access: Pateley Bridge is in Nidderdale 10 ½ miles south-west of Ripon on the B6265 and Yorke's Folly is set high on Guise Cliff 1 ½ miles to the south, accessible from Bewerley.

'Yorke's Folly', also known as 'The Stoops', comprises two ruined stone pillars built for John Yorke in the later eighteenth-century to provide work for the local unemployed. There was originally a third pillar but it tumbled down in 1893. The Yorke family owned nearby Bewerley Hall, just over the river from Pateley Bridge, which was in turn once the property of Fountains Abbey. The Abbey ruins may indeed have provided the inspiration for this mock ecclesiastical ruin.

Places of Interest in the Neighbourhood
55. Lady Clifford's Circular Almshouse
70. Nature's Curious Rock Carvings
80. A Cross for all Occasions
81. A French Village in Yorkshire

Yorke's Folly on Guise Cliff above Pateley Bridge.

69 Britain's most Beautiful Abbey

Position: Studley Royal (N Yorks)
O.S. Map: Northallerton, Ripon & surrounding area: Sheet No. 99
Map Ref: SE 284/686
Access: The Studley Royal Estate is 2 miles south-west of Ripon off the
B6265 Pateley Bridge road and is a National Trust property open all
year round except Fridays between November and January.

In the small museum at Fountains Abbey, which shares its boundary
with the Studley Royal estate, is an acoustic jar. This fairly unimpres-
sive curiosity, resembling a piece of ceramic drainpipe, is in fact a very

Monks Chapel on a hill near Fountains Abbey.

rare example of an early method of amplifying singing and music in the early church.

Fountains Abbey (SE 275/683) is the largest monastic ruin in Britain and contains the longest 'cellarium' (vaulted cellar) in Europe, being 300 feet long with 22 bays. The Abbey was founded in 1132 by 13 monks who seceded from the Benedictines at York Abbey, preferring the stricter Cistercian way of life. On the Dissolution of the Monasteries the Abbey was surrendered to the Crown in 1539. It was then bought by Sir Richard Gresham and sold to Sir Stephen Proctor in 1597 who built Fountains Hall using some of its now ruinous stone. It then passed to William Aislabie of nearby Studley Royal Manor (destroyed by fire in 1946) who together with his son John combined the two estates forming a park of some 650 acres. The two Aislabies completed the landscaping of the area using the River Skell to create the now world famous Studley Royal water gardens.

Access to the gardens can be gained at either end and a round walk shows it to be dotted with follies and curiosities. These include the Fishing Tabernacles, The Octagon Tower, the round Temple of Fame, Anne Boleyn's Seat, the Valley of the Seven Bridges, a ruined Chinese building, the Roman Pill Box and the double ice-houses. The Surprise View which affords a vista of the Abbey must be one of the finest viewpoints in Britain.

Half a mile south of the Abbey on How Hill is the eerie Monks Chapel (SE 275/671) built c.1200 and later restored. It is rumoured to have been used as a gambling den and is being restored by the National Trust. Access is not possible.

Places of Interest in the Neighbourhood
67. A Landowner's Lookout Tower
70. Nature's Curious Rock Carvings
71. An Anglo-Saxon Treasure House
72. A Medieval Fortified House
73. A Hall and a Famous Doorway

70 Nature's Curious Rock Carvings

Position: Brimham (N Yorks)
O.S. Map: Northallerton, Ripon & surrounding area: Sheet No. 99
Map Ref: SE 21/65
Access: Brimham Rocks are 8 miles south-west of Ripon on the B6265
Pateley Bridge road. It is a National Trust property open all year round
and access is on foot from the car park.

300 million years ago the area now known as Brimham Rocks was
a solid plateau of millstone grit and carboniferous limestone. Desert
sandstorms and thousands of years of subsequent erosion by ice, wind
and rain have resulted in a surrealistic landscape covering 360 acres, set
1,000 feet above sea level. The area is littered with hard gritstone out-
crops (or 'tors') eroded into fantastic shapes to which successive gener-
ations of visitors have given appropriate nicknames.

Best loved of all is the Dancing Bear but equally intriguing is the
Devil's Anvil, the Pulpit, the Idol Rock, the Tortoise, Rabbit,
Rhinoceros, Sphinx, Baboon's Head and Indian's Turban! Some are
easy to find whereas others are dependant upon the correct combina-
tion of light and shadow, as is the case with the fanciful Yoke of Oxen.
The Druid's Cave, Writing Desk and Altar reflect an ancient and
misplaced belief that the carvings were the work of Druids.

Next to a rock called the Crocodile is Brimham House, now an Infor-
mation Centre explaining this haunting geological phenomenon.

Places of Interest in the Neighbourhood
68. One Down, Two to Go!
69. Britain's Most Beautiful Abbey
72. A Medieval Fortified House
80. A Cross for all Occasions
81. A French Village in Yorkshire

71 An Anglo-Saxon Treasure House

Position: Ripon (N Yorks)
O.S. Map: Northallerton, Ripon & surrounding area: Sheet No. 99
Map Ref: SE 315/712
Access: Ripon is 9 miles north of Harrogate on the A61 and the crypt is
below the Cathedral of St Peter and St Wilfred in the town centre. It is
open to the public.

Ripon has a rare treasure beneath the Cathedral of St Peter and St
Wilfred – the Anglo-Saxon crypt. Crypts were used for the burial of
kings, as chapels and as treasuries, the one at Ripon until recently being
used to display valuable Church treasures. Its nickname 'The Needle'
refers to a narrow passage in one of the walls which may have been a
confessional. The vaulted crypt with its wall recess for oil lamps is the
only surviving part of an early church founded when Scottish monks set
up a community here in about 660. Within 10 years Abbot Wilfred
began building the church. Wilfred made several trips to Rome on foot,
from the last of which at the age of 70 he brought with him religious
relics for the church. The church, part of a Benedictine monastery, was
destroyed by the Danes in 950. It was followed by a Norman church in
the mid twelfth-century until the Puritans damaged it and the tower fell.
Not until 1836 was it restored and named the Cathedral of St Peter and
St Wilfred. Due to all this building activity the tower is now unique in
having two pointed arches and two rounded ones!

   Another crypt is the fine Norman one at St Mary's in Lastingham
(100: SE 728/904) 6 miles north-west of Pickering although, its pillar
bases suggest this too may be Anglo-Saxon. The church is on the site of
a monastery founded in 654, again damaged by the Danes and re-estab-
lished in 1078 by Stephen of Whitby. It is thus founded on one of the
earliest sacred places in England.

Places of Interest in the Neighbourhood
67. A Landowner's Lookout Tower
69. Britain's most Beautiful Abbey
72. A Medieval Fortified House
73. A Hall and a Famous Doorway
74. Where Yorkshire Barley became Yorkshire Beer

72 A Medieval Fortified House

Position: Markenfield (N Yorks)
O.S. Map: Northallerton, Ripon & surrounding area: Sheet No. 99
Map Ref: SE 295/674
Access: Markenfield Hall is 3 miles south-west of Ripon via a track
signposted 'Public Bridleway, Hell Wath Lane' running west from the
Ripley-Ripon A61, 1 ½ miles north of Wormald Green. It is privately
owned but open on Mondays from April to October.

Markenfield Hall is curious in being the one fortified manor in
Yorkshire which has survived more or less intact. It even escaped
damage during the Scots' incursion south after their victory at
Bannockburn, during which they burned Knaresborough. It was built
by John de Markinfield in 1310, and once included a drawbridge over
the moat. Today there is a stone bridge guarded by a gatehouse. It is an
L-shaped house, with outbuildings completing the square around a
central courtyard.

Places of Interest in the Neighbourhood
69. Britain's most Beautiful Abbey
71. An Anglo-Saxon Treasure House
73. A Hall and a Famous Doorway
80. A Cross for all Occasions

The gatehouse and moat at Markenfield Hall.

73 A Hall and a Famous Doorway

Position: Newby (N Yorks)
O.S. Map: Northallerton, Ripon & surrounding area: Sheet No. 99
Map Ref: SE 347/675
Access: Newby Hall is 4 miles south-east of Ripon on the B6265
Boroughbridge road and is open to the public between March 24th and
October 29th.

There are several curiosities at Newby Hall, itself a fine brick-built,
stone dressed house constructed in 1705 for Sir Edward Blackett of the
famous coal-mining family. Robert Adam was later responsible for the
lower wings on the east side as well as the lodge gates and for some
of the finest interiors in Europe. There are some excellent sculptures,
tapestries and Chippendale furniture as well as a replica collection of
the Crown Jewels.

The extensive grounds and fine gardens are bordered by the River
Ure. In the gardens can be found a mill (or 'gin') once turned by mule
and later by an engine.

Built into one of the garden walls one is surprised to find an original
door taken from Newgate Prison and re-erected here. It is the one
through which the legendary thief Jack Sheppard escaped on one of
four such occasions before being captured and hanged in 1724.

Curious also is the statue of a horseman. Originally a sculpture of the
King of Poland the original commissioner could not pay and it was
brought to England in 1675 by Sir Thomas Vyner. It was altered into
a statue of Charles II and erected in London before being moved to
Lincolnshire in 1779 and to Newby Hall in 1883.

Places of Interest in the Neighbourhood
69. Britain's most Beautiful Abbey
71. An Anglo-Saxon Treasure House
72. A Medieval Fortified House
74. Where Yorkshire Barley became Yorkshire Beer
75. The Devil's Arrows

74 Where Yorkshire Barley became Yorkshire Beer

Position: Langthorpe (N Yorks)
O.S. Map: Northallerton, Ripon & surrounding area: Sheet No. 99
Map Ref: SE 393/673
Access: Langthorpe is situated just north of Boroughbridge over the River Ure on the B6265 and the maltings are alongside the old railway line just before the village, down an unmarked track on the left.

Ale is made from pure water and malted barley to which hops can be added to produce beer. In medieval times brewing was a domestic concern undertaken by women and monks only. With the Dissolution of the Monasteries, the latter bequeathed Yorkshire its great brewing legacy and by the eighteenth-century those more skilful brewers were setting up small breweries to supply retail outlets. These became known as 'common brewers', such as the former Rhodes Brewery in Kirkgate, Thirsk. With the improved communication network made possible by the Industrial Revolution brewing became a fully commercialised concern, as at Malton and Tadcaster (see No. 4).

The heating of the water and malt is known as 'mashing' and the resultant 'wort' is then boiled and fermented in stone cisterns to produce the beer. The final taste is dictated by the water quality, brewing time and degree of malt curing. The process of malting enables the 'maltster' to use the starch in the barley seed (which feeds the young shoot until its roots grow) for its sugars, which ferment with the addition of yeast. To do this the barley is soaked and spread across a malting floor (or 'couch'). When the barley begins to sprout it is turned with a malt shovel and then taken to a kiln for drying to prevent further growth and to produce the flavour.

The county's oldest maltings are at Langthorpe and belonged to Warwick and Co's Anchor Brewery dated 1850. They are a three-storey structure with cast-iron columns and tie-bars to strengthen the floor supporting the wet barley during malting. At one end is a two-storey kiln with a curious conical brick flue more like an oasthouse.

Places of Interest in the Neighbourhood
71. An Anglo-Saxon Treasure House
72. A Medieval Fortified House
73. A Hall and a Famous Doorway
75. The Devil's Arrows

75 The Devil's Arrows

Position: Boroughbridge (N Yorks)
O.S. Map: Northallerton, Ripon & surrounding area: Sheet No. 99
Map Ref: SE 391/665
Access: Boroughbridge is 5½ miles south-west of Ripon on the A1. Just before the lane to Roecliffe passes below the A1 two of the arrows can be seen in the field on the right, and the third is beside the road on the left. View from the roadside if the fields are planted.

The Devil's Arrows are a group of 3 gritstone monoliths, or standing stones, about 20 feet high with a further 5 feet buried into the ground. There was originally a fourth but according to the antiquarian Camden, this was pulled down by treasure hunters in about 1582.

   The 3 stones are aligned approximately on a north-south axis and may have been connected with the prehistoric religious centre focused on the Thornborough-Hutton Moor area. This would make them of late Neolithic-Early Bronze Age in date and contemporary with Stonehenge in Wiltshire. In later times during the Summer solstice a fair was held in a nearby field, presumably echoing some ancient ritual once practised at the stones.

Places of Interest in the Neighbourhood
71. An Anglo-Saxon Treasure House
72. A Medieval Fortified House
73. A Hall and a Famous Doorway
74. Where Yorkshire Barley became Yorkshire Beer
77. The Source of a Great River

The 'Devil's Arrows' Standing stones at Boroughbridge.

76 Maiden's Garlands

Position: Alne (N Yorks)
O.S. Map: Malton, Pickering & surrounding area: Sheet No. 100
Map Ref: SE 495/653
Access: The village of Alne is 10 ½ miles north-west of York off the A19.

Inside St Mary's Church something rather unusual has survived on one of the walls. It is a floral maiden's garland, or crown, a curiosity to be found in Ashford-in-the-Water in Derbyshire and Abbott's Ann in Hampshire. However, this is one of Yorkshire's few examples (another is in the old St Stephen's church at Thorpe, south of Robin Hood's Bay), and with a date of 1709 it is one of the oldest surviving examples in the country. It is even more curious in being made of straw rather than the usual white paper or linen. In Shakespeare's *Hamlet* such crowns are called 'virgin crants' since they formed a funerary tribute to young women who died virgins and would never marry. The crowns were borne at the head of the funeral procession, often accompanied by a white glove, symbolizing pure clean hands, a handkerchief or collar and an inscription. Afterwards they were hung on the church wall. The reason for their survival is that it was thought unlucky to remove them. Instead they were allowed to gradually decay, fallen pieces were buried in the churchyard. This custom is thought to be Pre-Reformation in origin.

Just outside the village where the York road crosses Alne Avenue is a plague cross. Thought to have been erected during the 1604 plague, an inscription shows it was used later as a milestone. Food would have been left here by outsiders so as not to come into contact with the infected villagers, who in turn left money at the cross.

Places of Interest in the Neighbourhood
42. Amazing Mazes
43. A Very Odd Book Indeed
44. The Moving History of an Abbey!
74. Where Yorkshire Barley became Yorkshire Beer
75. The Devil's Arrows

77 The Source of a Great River

Position: Great Ouseburn (N Yorks)
O.S. Map: Northallerton, Ripon & surrounding area: Sheet No. 99
Map Ref: SE 449/618
Access: The village of Great Ouseburn is 11 miles north-west of York
on the A59/B6265 and the source stone is in a private garden behind the
grain store at a junction beyond.

The River Ouse, Yorkshire's most celebrated river, has been used as a
commercial waterway since Roman times. Its name is Celtic meaning
'water', hence there being several such named rivers in England. It is
some 55 miles in length from a junction of the insignificant Ouse Gill
Beck with the River Ure, down to the Humber estuary.

   Ouse Gill Beck rises in the village of Great Ouseburn where an ancient
inscribed stone pillar, known as the Source Stone, marks the start of the
river. Although no water can be seen around the pillar, the beck in fact
bubbles up from a spring nearby. Only when it joins the River Ure a
mile or so to the east does the river officially become the Ouse. North of
this point are the Rivers Ure and Swale, which join at Boroughbridge,
trailing far away up into the Yorkshire Dales. South of this point it
is the Ouse, which is joined by the Nidd (at Nun Monkton) which
flows down through York, Cawood (where the Wharfe joins), Selby and

The Source Stone of the River Ouse at Great Ouseburn.

Goole. By this time it has also been supplemented by the Derwent and Aire. Beyond, at Faxfleet, the River Trent joins and the mighty Ouse empties out into the sea through the Humber estuary.

Along its route there are only 2 short sections of canal with locks in order to bypass weirs. These are at Naburn (see No. 3) south of York, and Linton beyond. The Ouse is tidal as far as Naburn and this affects the size of boat using the river. The construction of a weir allowed vessels up to 140 feet long with a 24 feet beam to navigate as far as York, 45 miles from the river's mouth.

Places of Interest in the Neighbourhood
74. Where Yorkshire Barley became Yorkshire Beer
75. The Devil's Arrows
76. Maiden's Garlands
78. Petrifying Prophecies
79. Houses Hewn From Solid Rock

Objects being petrified under the Dropping Well at Knaresborough.

78 Petrifying Prophecies

Position: Knaresborough (N Yorks)
O.S. Map: Leeds, Bradford & Harrogate area: Sheet No. 104
Map Ref: SE 346/565
Access: Knaresborough is 3½ miles north-east of Harrogate on the A59. The Dropping Well Estate, for which there is an admission charge, is reached from the High Bridge which carries the A59 over the Nidd Valley.

Knaresborough's famous Dropping Well is reached via the pretty, tree-lined Long Walk alongside the river.

The Dropping Well is renowned for its ability to petrify objects dangled in its waters. The water drips down from a 30 feet high limestone overhang at the rate of 700 gallons an hour. Porous objects such as gloves, shoes and hats thus became impregnated with calcareous deposits and in less than a year can be removed as if fossilized into stone.

Nearby is a wishing well, but more curious is the prophetic Mother Shipton's Cave. Said to have been born here in 1488 her prophecies were not published until 1641. She moved to York marrying Toby Shipton, a carpenter, where she correctly predicted the downfall of Cardinal Wolsey (see No. 6) as well as the collapse of the original Knaresborough viaduct in 1848. The bridge was rebuilt and is the one still seen today, despite Mother Shipton saying it would fall a second time! It is also said she foresaw Castle Hill at Northallerton being 'filled with blood', and indeed the area later became a cemetery. Similarly, a road she predicted being built through the huge tithe barn at Ulleskelf-on-the-Wharfe without damage to the barn itself came true. The road was the York and North Midland railway and the barn was dismantled and rebuilt on a new site. Other claims attributed to Mother Shipton, such as the invention of cars and aeroplanes, were in fact the work of a Brighton bookseller last century!

Places of Interest in the Neighbourhood
77. The Source of a Great River
79. Houses Hewn from Solid Rock
80. A Cross for all Occasions
81. A French Village in Yorkshire
22. England's Largest Folly

79 Houses Hewn from Solid Rock

Position: Knaresborough (N Yorks)
O.S. Map: Leeds, Bradford & Harrogate area: Sheet No. 104
Map Ref: SE 352/564
Access: Knaresborough is 3 ½ miles north-east of Harrogate on the A59. The rock dwellings are cut into the Nidd Valley and are accessible from Abbey Road which starts at Low Bridge south of the town centre off the B6163.

The picturesque Nidd Valley, or crag as it is known, has in the past lent itself to some ambitious rock-cutting ventures.

In the east face of the valley can be found the House in the Rock, begun in 1770 by Thomas Hill, a weaver, and called Swallows' Nest. It was completed in 1786 by his son, who knighted himself Sir Thomas Hill and changed the name to Fort Montague. He even flew a flag from the battlements, printed his own banknotes and fired cannon salutes on public occasions.

Nearby is the comparatively sombre medieval rock-cut Chapel of Our Lady of the Crag (SE 353/563). Hewn by John the Mason in 1408, this wayside shrine is thought to be the third oldest of its type in Britain. Guarding the entrance is a figure thought by some to be St Robert whereas others think it is one of the Knights Templar, who were stationed at nearby Little Ribston. The chapel was renovated in 1916 when the figure of the Virgin and Child was installed. The name Abbey Road, which runs along the valley here, reflects the former existence of the Priory of St Robert, built in about 1250 a mile downriver. The saint had lived and died a hermit in St Robert's Cave (SE 362/562) near Grimbald Bridge, where he built a reputation for herbal cures and as a friend of the poor. The friars who succeeded him continued his work by raising money to pay ransoms for prisoners taken by the Saracens in the Crusades. However, the cave gained some notoriety in the mid-eighteenth century when schoolmaster Eugene Aram buried the body of his murdered lover here, for which he was hung in 1759.

Places of Interest in the Neighbourhood
77. The Source of a Great River
78. Petrifying Prophecies
80. A Cross for all Occasions
81. A French Village in Yorkshire
82. A Right Good Watering Hole!

80 A Cross for all Occasions

Position: Ripley (N Yorks)
O.S. Map: Northallerton, Ripon & surrounding area: Sheet No. 99
Map Ref: SE 283/605
Access: Ripley is 3½ miles north-west of Harrogate on the A61 and the 'Weeping Cross' is in All Saints Churchyard.

In and around the villages of North Yorkshire can be found an array of interesting ancient crosses, each with its own special purpose.

Some were 'Preaching Crosses' erected where missionaries first preached Christianity and are thus today close to where churches now stand. Others were 'Boundary Crosses', which marked out land owned by the monasteries.

Far rarer are 'Sanctuary Crosses' which marked the area inside which wrongdoers had the right to claim sanctuary. An example is the base of a sanctuary cross at Sharow (99: SE 324/720) east of Ripon.

More curious is the function of 'Weeping Crosses', which were set up in churchyards and beside the routes followed by funeral processions (they are also known as 'Cortege Crosses'). Around the base are hollow niches in which it has been suggested penitents knelt to pray. More likely votive offerings were placed here. The base of such a cross, with eight niches, is at Ripley (see above for access).

More common are 'Market Crosses'. In the Middle Ages, if a village was six miles or more from a market, it could apply to establish one of its own. When granted, a cross was often erected on the proposed site, usually a prominent position such as the square or green. There is a stepped market cross at Ripley, on the lowest step of which sat miscreants locked in the adjacent stocks. There is another at Redmire (98: SE 046/912) 4½ miles west of Leyburn. At Middleham (99: SE 127/877) 2½ miles south-east of Leyburn the cross is in two parts and it is said that traders sealed bargains by shaking hands in the space! Later some crosses became buildings in their own right (known as 'Butter Crosses') affording shelter to traders and providing an architectural focal point (see Beverley, No 14).

More ancient crosses include Lilla Cross (94: SE 889/985) on Fylingdales Moor, which is a 1,300 year old milestone. Undoubtedly the most artistic crosses belong to the Anglo-Saxon period, such as the seven feet high shaft outside the south porch of St Mary's church at Masham (99: SE 226/806) 8 miles north-west of Ripon. In St Andrew's Church at Middleton (100: SE 782/855) a mile north-west of Pickering is the so-called 'Warrior Cross'. However one of the finest pieces of Anglo-Saxon work is a cross found at St Agatha's church at Easby (92: NZ 185/003) a mile south-east of Richmond. A cast is now on display as the original is in the Victoria and Albert Museum.

Places of Interest in the Neighbourhood
70. Nature's Curious Rock Carvings
72. A Medieval Fortified House
78. Petrifying Prophecies
79. Houses Hewn from Solid Rock
81. A French Village in Yorkshire
82. A Right Good Watering Hole!

The penitents Weeping Cross at Ripley.

81 A French Village in Yorkshire

Position: Ripley (N Yorks)
O.S. Map: Northallerton, Ripon & surrounding area: Sheet No. 99
Map Ref: SE 283/605
Access: Ripley is 3½ miles north-west of Harrogate on the A61 and Ripley Castle estate is open to the public.

Ripley village today is very different from the original one as a result of Sir William Ingilby, of Ripley Castle, eccentrically rebuilding the whole place in 1827-28. He created a new 'model village' of terraces in the local stone, and built to resemble a village in Alsace-Lorraine. The largest building, the village hall, was heavily decorated in the Alsatian style and was called the 'Hotel de Ville'. Not content with this Sir William called his own castle 'Das Schloss'! To confuse the matter further the sentry box bears the inscription 'Parlez au Suisse', reminding visitors to inform the lodgekeeper of their arrival – but why Swiss?

The land on which the castle stands was given to Thomas Ingilby after saving King Edward III from a wild boar. During the Civil War and following the Battle of Marston Moor Oliver Cromwell stayed at the castle for a night. This was in spite of the hostility of Royalist Sir William Ingilby's wife who took up guard with two pistols. There are bullet holes in a wall at Ripley where some villagers were executed by Cromwell's men at this time.

The gardens were set out by Capability Brown and it was Sir William Ingilby who dammed the River Nidd to form the attractive lake.

Places of Interest in the Neighbourhood
70. Nature's Curious Rock Carvings
72. A Medieval Fortified House
78. Petrifying Prophecies
79. Houses Hewn from Solid Rock
80. A Cross for all Occasions
82. A Right Good Watering Hole!

The village of Ripley.

82 A Right Good Watering Hole!

Position: Harrogate (N Yorks)
O.S. Map: Leeds, Bradford and Harrogate: Sheet No. 104
Map Ref: SE 31/55
Access: Harrogate is 19 miles west of York on the A59 and its famous
spa wells are dotted around the town.

Harrogate is no longer what Dickens described as 'the queerest place',
but like any town with a history it still has its fair share of curiosities.

On Harlow Hill, on the B6162 running south-west out of Harrogate, is
Harlow Hill Tower (SE 288/542). This is a plain, square stone structure
built in 1829 by John Thompson as an observatory. Although it was
opened to the public in 1900 it didn't achieve its original purpose until
1933. Standing in a public park, it gives good views all round, although
a local saying that you can see Helvellyn on a fine day is probably
wishful thinking!

Harrogate's chief claim to fame rested, between the discovery of 'The
Tewit Well' in 1571 and the closing of the Royal Baths in 1969, on its
medieval springs and wells to which crowds flocked hoping to be cured
from all manner of ills. Famous in the seventeenth-century, and even
more so in Victorian and Edwardian times, the town popularised the
mixture of medicine and social life. 'The Tewit Well' may have been
named after the local term for a lapwing, which were seen here in great
numbers by William Slingsby when out riding.

Harrogate was soon dubbed a Spa town, or Spaw in the north of
England, by Dr Timothy Bright after a similar site at Spa in Belgium.
Harrogate's oldest spring is the so-called 'Chalybeate Spring' which
refers to the type of water. In all there are more than 80 springs, some
chalybeate, some sulphurous and some limestone - indeed it has probably the highest concentration and variety of such waters in the world!

Before being enclosed and pumped the springs ran free creating boggy
areas. For example St John's Well on Wetherby Road, also called
'Sweet Spaw', was originally just a basin with a simple roof. Gradually
it developed into an elaborate pavilion, but it retained a free tap outside
for those who couldn't pay the entry fee!

The Royal Pump Room, which covers the old 'Sulphur Well', was
responsible for ensuring Harrogate's fame as a spa and entertainment
centre in Victorian times, and now contains a museum. The Royal
Bath Assembly Rooms (1897) was once one of the world's largest
hydrotherapy centres and is still redolent of older, more elegant days.

Other curiosities include a plaque marking the formation of the world's first bicycle touring club (1878); the 200 acre open space known as 'The Stray', declared open forever in 1770; a tree on Victoria Avenue which is the sole survivor of Knaresborough forest; a nine feet tall turnpike boundary stone for the Leeds-Ripon turnpike; and Hales Bar where gas lamps and cigar lighters still burn as of yore.

Places of Interest in the Neighbourhood
78. Petrifying Prophecies
79. Houses Hewn from Solid Rock
80. A Cross for all Occasions
81. A French Village in Yorkshire

The pavilion over St John's Well in Harrogate.

Index

Places by Page Number

The Curiosities of England

The following titles in the series have already been published and can be ordered at all bookshops, or in case of difficulties direct from the publishers.

Buckinghamshire Curiosities John Lucas 1 874336 11 3

Cheshire Curiosities Peter Bamford 0 946159 96 3

Cotswold Curiosities Reginald Dixon 0 946159 51 1

Dorset Curiosities George Osborn 0 946159 38 6

East Anglian Curiosities Rick O'Brien 0 946159 97 1

Hampshire Curiosities Jo Daper 0 946159 57 2

Hertfordshire Curiosities John Lucas 0 946159 75 0

Isle of Wight Curiosities Jack Jones 0 946159 67 X

Kent Curiosities John Vigar 0 946159 95 5

Northamptonshire Curiosities Chris Billing 1 874336 12 1

North and East Yorkshire Curiosities Duncan & Trevor Smith 1 874336 09 1

Nottinghamshire Curiosities Geoffrey Oldfield 0 946159 98 X

Somerset Curiosities Enid Byford 0 946159 48 3

South and West Yorkshire Curiosities Duncan & Trevor Smith 0 946159 99 8